674

Group Spiritual Direction: Community For Discernment

"Two people, three people, ten people may be in living touch with one another through (God) who underlies their separate lives....We know that these souls are with us, lifting their lives and ours continually to God and opening themselves, with us, in steady and humble service to (God)."[1]

Thomas Kelly

Rose Mary Dougherty, S.S.N.D.

PAULIST PRESS
New York/Mahwah, N.J.

Cover design by James F. Brisson
Cover art: The cover sketch was designed by Peter Gray as a memorial card for Lowell Glendon, S.S. When he was dying of cancer, Lowell said that he didn't want many people around him. Instead, he wanted "only a few faithful friends who could pray me to God." Lowell's words, so powerfully illustrated by Peter Gray's sketch, capture the essence of spiritual community for the author.

Library of Congress Cataloging-in-Publication Data

Dougherty, Rose Mary, 1939-
      Group spiritual direction : community for discernment / by Rose Mary Dougherty.
        p. cm.
      Includes bibliographical references and index.
      ISBN 0-8091-3598-1 (alk. paper)
      1. Spiritual direction. 2. Church group work. 3. Discernment of spirits. I. Title.
BV5053.D68   1995   95-203356
a253.5'3—dc20   CIP

Published by Paulist Press
997 Macarthur Boulevard
Mahwah, New Jersey 07430

Printed and bound in the
United States of America

Contents

Appreciations

I dedicate this book with affection and gratitude to Susie Dillon, Sue Parker, Lynne Smith, Paula Endo, Bill Plitt, and Marcia Brewington—participants in the first group spiritual direction I offered—whose desire for God led them into uncharted territory with strangers who later became spiritual friends.

Acknowledgements

I am grateful to Ray and the many who have encouraged me and prayed for me throughout the writing of this book and those who read my work in various phases of its development and offered feedback: John Becker, Ph.D., Director of the Willingness Center in Washington, DC; Marianne Boehm, S.C., spiritual director and writer; Mary Ellen Dougherty, SSND, spiritual director and writer; The Reverend Lloyd Edwards, Episcopal priest, pastoral counselor and spiritual director; The Reverend Tilden Edwards, Episcopal priest, Executive Director of Shalem Institute, spiritual director and author; Christine Elliott, United Methodist pastor and facilitator for group spiritual direction; Michael Fonseca, LSW, long time associate of Anthony de Mello; Natalie Ganley, Roman Catholic spiritual director and writer; Patricia Glinka, SSND, Roman Catholic pastoral associate; William Hug, Ph.D., Presbyterian pastor and pastoral counselor; Gregory Mestanas, Ph.D, psychologist; Virginia Niemeyer, Roman Catholic pastoral associate; Maria Rieckelman, Maryknoll Sister and psychiatrist; Lynne Smith, participant and facilitator in group spiritual direction; Sharon Smith, Unitarian Universalist participant in group spiritual direction; Eleanor Stonebraker, lay reader for the Evangelical Lutheran Church, spiritual director and author; Theodore Tracy, S.J., spiritual director and author.

Finally, and most especially, I want to thank Gerald May, Monica Maxon, and Clare Openshaw who accompanied me to the end of this writing.

Introduction

I am writing this for those individuals who have an appreciation of spiritual direction and want to offer spiritual direction for themselves and others in a group setting. Though formal background in the theory and practice of spiritual direction may make the contents of this book more accessible to the reader, such background is not essential. While I have chosen not to include an in-depth study of spiritual direction within this work, I do intend to provide the insight into my understanding of spiritual direction necessary to substantiate my approach to group spiritual direction.[1]

Background Experience

To begin, I would like to share some of the experiences which have helped shape my understanding and practice of group spiritual direction. For the past twenty-five years I have received spiritual direction; I have offered spiritual direction at least informally for twenty years. At the beginning of those twenty years I was certain that I knew little about spiritual direction—what it was, how it happened. I had no training, but I was willing to trust my experience of receiving direction to serve me well with others.

Now, twenty years later, I have had even more experience: two years of serious study of spiritual direction in an ecumenical program for spiritual directors and seventeen years on the staff of the same program at The Shalem Institute for Spiritual

1

Formation; one year of internship for spiritual direction in a retreat setting, eighteen years in a colleague group for spiritual directors, frequent facilitation of groups in which moments of spiritual direction occurred, and many hours in retreat and ongoing spiritual direction, my own and others. Despite or because of this experience and learning, I am less certain about what I do or do not know about spiritual direction. I have learned that I can trust only the presence of God to serve me well in this adventure.

I have finally come to realize that while authentic spiritual direction has something to do with a sense of calling for those who participate in it, the real "success" in spiritual direction is not dependent upon my skills as a director or upon the spiritual sophistication of those who come for spiritual direction. Rather, the critical element in spiritual direction, which those involved share, is the intention to rely on God, to seek God actively and wait for God's leading. Where this can happen, between two individuals or within groups, hearts are opened, private agendas are put on hold and God's Spirit is given free rein.

Having experienced first-hand the fruit of this looking to God which I call prayerfulness, I began to sense the potential for ongoing spiritual direction of individuals within group settings. I was aware that people at the Shalem Institute and elsewhere were offering groups that included spiritual conversation and times of spiritual direction. I was also aware that at least some people in these groups wanted more time for the articulation of their spiritual journeys than such groups could provide. I wanted to experiment with a group whose primary focus would be spiritual direction.

Eight years ago I shared my ideas with people who had been part of Shalem groups for several years. From those who expressed an interest, I selected six people to participate in a year of group spiritual direction with me as their facilitator. These people were very diverse in their theologies and none of them had been in spiritual direction before. But each had an earnest desire for God, a readiness to be present for one another in the exploration of that desire, and a willingness to pray for one another.

None of us knew exactly what our time together would look like, though I had images of what I thought it should be. Fortunately the sensitivity of the group to God's leading overrode my compulsions to try to shape our time according to my image. We grew together in our availability to God for one another. Although as a facilitator I did not share my spiritual journey directly with the group, I found then that I was held in the womb of prayer by the prayerfulness of other participants. I also found that my spiritual heart was often addressed through the wisdom offered to another participant.

Since that first year's experiment, this group has been meeting without me for seven years, rotating the role of facilitator and allowing space after each session to reflect on what has gone on among them, and to share their perceptions of this with one another. Originally, to ease their fears of losing what they had gained in the first year, I agreed to be with them several times. But this was never needed. They grew to trust God's presence with them and to appreciate the gift of their presence together. There has seldom been a time when anyone is absent. As they grow together as spiritual friends, they are reluctant to meet as a group for anything other than spiritual direction lest they jeopardize the freedom of the group.

Three members of this group and two other people now work with me as facilitators for new groups. Once a month, at the end of the small group sessions which we facilitate, we meet to become spiritual directors for one another as we recount our sense of God and our openness or resistance to God during our time of facilitating. These people have become not only my spiritual directors but also my teachers. I know there is still much to learn from them. They have taught me mostly about humility and a purity of heart that struggles to seek God first even at the risk of appearing unknowledgeable or incompetent. They do not stand behind credentials of any kind. Although they have had more experience with group spiritual direction than others in the group and are willing to offer the gift of their experience to the group, they do not seem to get caught up in roles as easily as I do. Rather they are simply there as themselves, wanting to trust God in the transient uneasiness of their not knowing, willing to learn, to be changed through the process of the group interaction.

Learning from the Tradition of Spiritual Community

In choosing to offer spiritual direction in a group setting, I was aware of entering a rich tradition in which individuals have valued the spiritual community of small groups as a means of nourishment for their spiritual lives. Although these groups may have differed in the focus of their attention, depending upon the current understanding of spirituality and the perceived needs of members, such groups have offered valuable insights for spiritual community and thus for group spiritual direction.

My own practice of group spiritual direction has heightened my appreciation for the essence of spiritual community found in such groups. Conversely, this growing appreciation for spiritual community has strongly influenced my approach to group spiritual direction. Thus I find it necessary to situate group spiritual direction within the context of spiritual community before talking about spiritual direction and discernment.

In writing about spiritual community, I hope to present what I sense to be at the heart of spiritual community. I will cite examples which elaborate on this consideration. While I will include the historical background necessary to make sense of these examples, I do not claim to be an historian or to be offering a comprehensive history of spiritual community.

Written Resources

The perusal of current literature about group spiritual direction, sparse as it is, has also been a part of my preparation for this writing. I cite only the works that have contributed most to the clarification and articulation of my concept of group spiritual direction. I am especially indebted to Lisa Meyers for her unpublished manuscript entitled, "Spiritual Guidance and Small Groups in the Presbyterian and Reformed Tradition."[2]

Her paper came to me at a time when I was beginning to question the need for a book on this topic since I had been imparting the "oral tradition" of group spiritual direction through annual workshops for several years. In opening new areas of relevance for group spiritual direction to me, Lisa's paper encouraged me to offer my ideas to a wider audience than those who might attend a workshop. Thus, her work prodded me to persevere in writing this book.

Donna Lord, a graduate of Shalem's Spiritual Guidance Program, has written about how she incorporated group spiritual direction within the context of a contemplative prayer group.[3] Kathleen Fischer devotes a chapter of her book, *Women at the Well*, to her understanding of group spiritual direction and its congruence with the felt need of women to have the companionship of other women in their journeys. Her work offers practical assistance in beginning group spiritual direction.[4] In his chapter in a collective work entitled *The Art of Clinical Supervision*, Lowell Glendon, one-time staff member of The Loyola Institute of Pastoral Studies, proposes group spiritual direction as a viable mode of supervision among members of retreat teams and spiritual directors. The process he describes is similar to that used by Shalem in colleague groups of peer supervision, a process designed to provide group spiritual direction for spiritual directors around their relationships of spiritual direction.[5]

Many writings in Quaker spirituality[6] and George Montague's work on the theology of the Holy Spirit[7] have given me valuable insight into the vital roles of trust and attention to the Holy Spirit in group settings for discernment. The Quaker literature especially has reinforced my sense of the need to include substantial periods of silence in such settings. This silence is both a means of drawing the group into prayer for one another and of honoring God's Spirit as the primary spiritual director for each person in the group.

Finally, writings on group theory and group skills, especially those by David and Frank Johnson, Rodney Napier and Matti Gershenfeld, and Irvin Yalom, have sharpened for me distinctions between spiritual direction groups and other growth groups.[8] These readings have increased my knowledge of the range of group dynamics that could be applicable to the process of group spiritual direction. My experience with group spiritual direction, however, has strengthened my conviction that knowledge of group theory, while sometimes useful, has very little direct bearing on the efficacy of group spiritual direction.

Evolution of the Process of Group Spiritual Direction

I continue to reflect on my experience of group spiritual direction in various settings and on my conversations with the women who are now facilitators with me. I have discussed with others their understandings of spiritual direction and group theory as well as their exploration of group spiritual direction. These combined resources have not relieved my state of unknowing. Rather, they have confirmed the necessity of unknowing for entering with trust into the venture of group spiritual direction. Thus they have helped me shape an evolving process of group spiritual direction. This process honors both the unknowing and the knowing I have about spiritual direction. It also acknowledges the need for a structure to assist spiritual direction in a group setting.

The Intent of This Book

The following pages are a distillation of my learnings. Although I include a very detailed description of the process I use in group spiritual direction I do not intend this book as a handbook. Instead, I hope it will be a catalyst for your reflection on what might best serve your understanding of spiritual direction and an encouragement for you to experiment with group spiritual direction in settings that seem ripe for this.

Chapter 1

Spiritual Community:
The Ambiance for Group
Spiritual Direction

"The crowd seated around Jesus told him, 'Your mother and your brothers and sisters are outside asking for you.' He replied, 'Who are my mother and my brothers?' And looking at those sitting in a circle around him he continued, 'Here are my mother and my brothers. Anyone who does the will of God, that person is my brother and sister and mother.'"

Mark 3:32-35[1]

The Essence of Spiritual Community

In this passage, Jesus is suggesting that the bond of spiritual community is a common wanting to do the will of God. Those who gather with him in this seeking are his family. They are the ones who nourish his life of authenticity with God.

This view of spiritual community is foundational to my understanding of spiritual direction. Not only is spiritual community the ambiance in which spiritual direction occurs, but also spiritual direction is often the means through which spiritual community is most clearly recognized and claimed. The blessing of reciprocity present in the bond of spiritual community is one of the fruits of genuine spiritual direction.

Paul and others in the early church acknowledged the bond of seeking and sharing which marks spiritual community. This is evidenced in their frequent use of the term "fellowship" to describe the community of believers. This word had its roots in the Greek "koinonia" which means "an intimate bond of sharing that is established by participation in a shared reality."[2] Thich Nhat Hanh, a Vietnamese Buddhist monk, speaks of this participation as the principle of "interbeing": "The one is many, and the many are the one." He says, "To be is to inter-be. We cannot just be by ourselves alone. We have to inter-be with every other thing."[3] Teilhard de Chardin affirms this truth when he says of human beings, "Driven by the forces of love, the fragments of the world seek each other so that the world may come into being."[4]

Spiritual community—our being in relationship with others, moving toward fullness in God together—is the way things really are. This is our shared reality, despite experiences to the contrary such as loneliness, betrayal, and war. Fortunately there have always been Truth seekers, Love seekers, God seekers who have acknowledged this reality and have tried to give expression to it. In the practice of Buddhism, for instance, one is reminded frequently of the Sangha, the community of fellow pilgrims—past and present—who walk the road with us. We are encouraged to seek refuge in the Sangha just as surely as we seek refuge in the Buddha who is our Inner Teacher, and in the Teachings. This taking refuge in the Sangha is not meant to replace our personal responsibility. Rather, it is to open us to the support we need to travel alone with our Inner Teacher.[5] Likewise Christian tradition has given much attention to the concept of the communion of saints, the community of all those living and deceased who want God and are praying for one another to be faithful in that wanting.

Vowed Community

There have been people in various religious traditions whose spiritual commitment has led them to choose within the Sangha or the communion of saints a more visible spiritual community. In making such a choice they sought to participate in a rule of life and common practices with others who shared their commitment. Monastic life, and later vowed religious community, provided options for such choices. This way of life was not only intended to encourage those within its structures; it also was meant to be a living reminder and expression of what every person is ultimately called to, a radical commitment to God.[6]

As religious life became more widespread, many began to see the living of a radical commitment as possible only within the confines of religious life. They viewed the command to "seek God first" and the subsequent need for support in this endeavor as applicable only to this small number of vowed persons. They saw these vowed people as standing before God, living a dedicated life in the stead of everyone else. Some church authorities even discouraged "ordinary people" from taking their spiritual lives too seriously lest, in their concern for the spiritual life, they become dissatisfied with their commonplace lives and the duties attached to them.

Eventually, however, such authorities recognized once again what was later to be called "the universal call to holiness."[7] With that recognition they asserted that holiness was possible within the context of the daily life of all. As people outside religious communities consciously began to seek this holiness, they looked for the support of a personal, visible community to assist them which was not always available within the institutional church. Through the centuries, various forms of community have arisen to meet this need. My reflection on such communities has heightened my awareness of the need to ground group spiritual direction in an understanding of spiritual community.

Other Spiritual Communities

The Acts of the Apostles describes the community of the early followers of Jesus:

They remained faithful to the teaching of the apostles, to the brotherhood, to the breaking of the bread and to the prayers…Each day, with one heart, they regularly went to the temple but met in their houses for the breaking of the bread; they shared their food gladly and generously; they praised God and were looked up to by everyone.[8]

Later, other such communities were founded among smaller circles of believers. One such community was that founded by Marcella in 352 A.D. Inspired by earlier models of monasticism, she "gathered about her a band of like-minded women who met for scripture study in her home." Many of these women subsequently used their own palaces for the practice of monastic life.[9]

In 1607, Francis de Sales, a Roman Catholic priest who spent much of his time supporting lay persons in the living of the spiritual life, encouraged and assisted them to find spiritual companions for the journey. To them he wrote: "For those who live in the world and desire to embrace true virtue it is necessary to unite together in holy sacred friendship. By this means they encourage, assist, and lead one another to embrace true virtue."[10]

Also in the early 1600s, priests of the Society of Jesus, who had been giving retreats to lay people, saw the need for support among retreatants if they were to integrate the experience of the retreat with their daily lives. With this in mind, these Jesuits established small communities where people might intentionally inspire one another in their devotion to God and service to others. These communities also claimed a common mission of the group to assist the church with its needs. Such groups continue today as Christian Life Communities.[11]

Similar in intent is the permanent Group Reunion which is an ongoing follow-up to the experience of the Cursillo, a three-day retreat of encounter with Christ. The Cursillo movement began in Spain in 1949. It continues as a viable means of renewal especially for those who participate in the weekly accountability meeting of the Group Reunion.[12]

The Group Reunion reflects something of the spirit of accountability groups that were begun by John Wesley, founder of Methodism, and that exist today in various modified forms. Early in the development of his spiritual sensitivity, John Wesley recognized the importance of community for his growth. While in Oxford in 1729, he gathered around him a small group of men who shared his desire to give themselves completely to God and who were willing to hold one another accountable for a style of living consonant with that desire. Some years later he participated in a similar group with the Moravians. The nurturing he received from these groups prompted him to incorporate such groups within Methodism.[13]

Expanding on his own experience, John Wesley organized the general membership of Methodism into classes that provided a structure for "prayer, instruction, mutual confession and support." He urged those more familiar with the spiritual life to join smaller groups or bands whose weekly meetings began and ended with prayer and provided the opportunity "for each member to speak freely and plainly the true state of our souls." Of the interaction of the group, Wesley said, "Every person in the band is my monitor and I his; else I know of no use of our being in a band."[14]

In recent years David Watson, a Wesleyan scholar, has experimented with a modification of the class meeting and is offering a new model to congregations as Covenant Discipleship groups. While making provisions for particular spiritual needs of participants, these groups are faithful to the Wesleyan notion of accountability to a prescribed covenant and maintain the principle of "fraternal admonition" or the giving of "earnest advice" as part of their accountable discipleship.[15]

Recently, John R. Martin, of the Anabaptist tradition, has also devoted attention to the revitalization of the understanding and practice of discipleship and admonition within his tradition. Martin describes biblical discipleship as "a dynamic following of the risen Christ, not following a predefined order." For him, at the heart of discipleship is a personal relationship with the risen Christ, rather than one's capacity to follow a set of rules. From this perspective, admonition is the means by which one is assisted in recognizing the unique ways of God's leading in one's life and in becoming accountable to live in faithful response to that leading. "The primary task of the person doing the admonishing is to help the other person live the truth God has shown him or her, not to dictate the details of their life or to enforce a defined order."[16]

Marlene Kropf, a Mennonite, said, "A dearth of opportunities for companionship or friendship leaves people singularly ill-equipped today for growth toward spiritual maturity. If Pascal's dictum is true ('One Christian is no Christian'), then a key to renewal in the church (and in the salvation of the world) is the restoration of vigorous communities of faith for the purpose of discipling."[17]

Other denominations as well are acknowledging the need for small communities among their members. In 1989, the Presbyterian Church, USA reaffirmed the central role of community for nurturing growth in the life of Christian faith in the Reformed Tradition.[18] The Roman Catholic Church in the United States also is looking to small Christian communities as a corrective for the large impersonal structures that have become local churches. Through parish-wide programs such as Christ Renews His Church, people have experienced that "small Christian communities can provide an effective way for inviting large numbers of parishioners to understand and concretize the grace of holiness in their own lives."[19]

The Society of Friends has always upheld the unique place of spiritual community, particularly in individual discernment: "Each of us has an inner, divine light that gives us the guidance we need but is often obscured by sundry forms of inner and outer interference." The Quaker Meeting encourages people to pay attention to this inner guidance. Within the Meeting there is sometimes a more intimate gathering, the Clearness Committee. This group of people gathers together to "help people discover their own God-given leadings and callings through silence, through questioning, through listening, through prayer." Although the Clearness Committee is not an ongoing gathering of the same people as are most of the communities mentioned here, it reflects the heart of spiritual community.[20]

The Heart of Spiritual Community

What is the heart of spiritual community? What draws people to spiritual community? I think Jesus helped people name this for themselves: "What do you want? What are you looking for?"[21] Benedict, founder of an early monastic community, was very direct in asking that question of those who came to join his community: "Do you seek God?" That, in fact, was the foundation of his community. In his rule he says of admitting members, "The concern must be if the novice seeks God."[22]

This God-seeking is ideally the ground of all those who are searching for spiritual community. Our searching, our wanting is reflective of God's seeking of us and God's dream for community planted in us. Jesus prays his prayer for "oneing" in us: "May they all be one, may they be one as we are one."[23]

Every once in a while we meet (perhaps are given by God) another person or group of kindred spirits where for a brief period of time we have a glimpse into the way things could be, the community to which we are really called. In that setting our desire for God comes alive, and we feel supported in our desire by the person or the group. Even though we might not ever see them again, we know that there is something that we've "touched into" together. The essence of what we have "touched into" continues to be with us, nurturing our desire long after we are separated.

Unfortunately today, because there is so much isolation and loneliness, people often get confused about what they're looking for. They are unable to discriminate between the companionship of interested people and the community of people who can help them seek God. Spiritual community makes real our seeking and it supports us in the seeking. This is what is at the heart of spiritual community.

In spiritual community, there is a bonding that goes beyond human expectations. It is a bonding of prayer and spiritual caring that is not dependent on the externals of similar personalities, tastes, or causes. Spiritual community is more than a feeling of warmth and comfort that comes in knowing that there are people with whom we can easily share the content of our lives, people on whom we can depend to meet our needs and alleviate our suffering. When those aspects of community are not present, we can think we are lacking community. In fact, that which is essential for spiritual community, the respect for our relationship with God, may really be present for us. At times the strength of spiritual community lies in the love of people who refrain from getting caught in the trap of trying to fix everything for us, who pray for us and allow us the pain of our wilderness, our wants, so that we might become more deeply grounded in God.

The Demands of Spiritual Community

Spiritual community, then, both fosters and demands the asceticism of radical love, a love which we can only pray for and be open to receiving. It is characterized by a single-mindedness, a love of God that encompasses and directs our love of others. It is a love that we gradually grow into as we pray for an attitude of intercessory prayer.

The attitude of intercessory prayer is a willingness to enter into God's prayer in us, the caring love of God for ourselves, for others. In this place of prayer, as we become sensitized to God's unique invitations to us as participants in that love, we may be called to let go of some of our vested interests and our traditional ways of caring for other people. Presence and absence, silence and words, doing and not doing all become relativized against the backdrop of God's prayer in us. As that prayer becomes realized in the community, old norms for community disappear. A new dynamism shows itself which can be neither predicted nor controlled by those involved. Hearts are freed for an authentic love which embraces all of creation. We come to cherish the spiritual community of which we are a part.

Spiritual direction is one expression of spiritual community. The dynamism of radical love that animates spiritual community also animates spiritual direction in any form. In spiritual direction two or more people gather in the power of love and for the sake of love. In the arena of love, one is brought face-to-face with the primary discernment of spiritual community: "Do you seek God?" And then, "What does this seeking mean for your life?"

Chapter 2

Spiritual Direction

"The spiritual director has the responsibility of intercessory prayer, of staying in God's presence on behalf of the person in order that there may be divine light in his direction."

Elizabeth O'Connor[1]

Participation in the Spiritual Life

Ideally in spiritual direction, two people (or more in group spiritual direction) experience God drawing them together precisely to pay attention to love, the prayer of God unfolding in the heart of the person seeking spiritual direction. This prayer of God, really God's yearning for the person, has long been prayed before the person comes for spiritual direction.

Whether or not one is aware of it, God is constantly engaged with the human heart. God is present, inviting, cajoling, challenging, enabling, always loving persons to be who they are—lovers at home in Love. At some point in the spiritual journey we are awakened to this love affair and the subsequent choice to claim the primacy of love in our lives. For some this may show itself as an insatiable passion for truth or for justice, for others it may be a deep reverence for beauty, and still for others it may appear as the drawing of the heart to compassionate service. Others may sense only that beneath the pain, the joy, the complacency of their lives there is a Reality which can no longer be ignored. However this longing shows itself, it is ultimately a longing for God. This longing for God is the bedrock of the spiritual life and of spiritual direction.

There may be other supports for the spiritual life, other than spiritual direction. Membership in a local church or some other group may regularly present people with spiritual imperatives and nourish them in patterns of authentic living, but this participation is not always sufficient. Nor is our ongoing personal prayer necessarily sufficient. Though our prayer honors God's love and sensitizes us to its steady hold on our lives, we often miss the subtle nuances of its varied daily expressions. With the best of intentions we don't always make loving choices. When we realize this, we may look for a place where we can be accountable for our love. We may search within our church community or elsewhere for a group or a person who can assist us in the noticing and can support us in the loving. Though we may not name it as such, we are seeking what traditionally has been known as spiritual direction.

One participant in group spiritual direction at the Shalem Institute wrote about it in his church bulletin:

I experienced a powerful shift in my relationship with God during those months in group spiritual direction. I moved from an encumbered, rigid, self-centered approach to an awareness of the potential for one more God-centered. I began to see a range in my daily experience from the simple—increased awareness of God's hand in nature, the flowers, the trees and birds—to more complex revelations of the Spirit at work. With these deeper encounters with God, I gained understanding, for example, in the meaning of an experience with a colleague, friend, or family member. I found new direction for being with God in that relationship. This reorientation was the time for discovering God as the source of love.

Now that the experience at Shalem has ended, I feel a void. I miss the new orientation acquired through group spiritual direction. There are many Sundays when I walk away from the church without the feeling of God being present for me. I have discovered there is more to worshiping the Lord than only through one weekly encounter. God seems often not to be present for me there because I am pre-occupied with my own space. I find myself daily slipping back to the old orientation of my life and away from the discipline of study, meditation, and worship. I seek to join with others in our church community who may wish to explore the search for a heightened relationship with God and a more responsible love for others.

Spiritual Direction: Why Seek It?

This participant is describing what often brings people to spiritual direction. It is similar to what prompted me to look for it. In my own case, as a vowed member of a religious congregation, I found that our rule of life supported me in the daily discipline of study, meditation, and worship. However, I found this was not enough. Structures of religious life were changing, opening new avenues for ministry and for personal decision-making. I felt ill-equipped for such new-found responsibility. I needed someone who could help me look at my choices in light of my relationship with God.

At the time, it didn't occur to me to pray about this. I felt the need for immediate help so I went to the only person in my area that I knew to be a spiritual guide. Since that time, I have come to a fuller understanding of how to choose such a person. My experience and that of others has convinced me that if God is in my felt need for spiritual direction, then it is safe to assume that God will assist me in finding the resource I need. It is also safe to assume that God will invite into spiritual direction with me the person I need to be my spiritual director.[2]

At the time, the director I approached, being more experienced than I, suggested that we pray, together and separately, to know if God was bringing us together. He also suggested that we try to recall any sense of fitness or appropriateness that was there during our initial conversation as well as any questions that arose. We would test this recollection in prayer as we asked, "What is your desire for us now in this consideration?" I was impatient to get on with the relationship, but he preferred that we wait for mutual clarity or at least some indication that we move ahead in trust. I felt that we should move ahead because of my sense of ease in speaking with him about what was important to me. Also he was the only director I knew. He insisted that there were other directors available, offered some names, but he also said he felt comfortable with moving ahead. For him the indication was his sense of prayer when we were together. We agreed, however, to check out the rightness of our continuing together from time to time.

We worked out of what I later came to recognize as a classical model of spiritual direction.[3] We met regularly, usually once a month, for about an hour, to focus specifically on my spiritual life, God's invitations moving in me and my responses. Early on, the director had asked me what I was looking for in spiritual direction. I had read some material on discernment and had some immediate decisions to make, so I said I wanted help with discernment. Later I realized that what I really wanted was answers from him. I became frustrated when answers were not forthcoming. I remember the last time I pushed him for an answer. Three times I had asked, "What do *you* think about this?" All three times he reversed the question. Finally I blurted out, "I don't know what I think. If I did I wouldn't be asking you!" His response was simple: "Then maybe you need to spend some time in prayer to see what God might have to say to you. After all, the Holy Spirit is really your director. I'm only here to help you listen to the Spirit speaking within you. Why don't you pray about it and see what your life has to say to you about it? We can talk about it again next month if you want to."

Dynamics of the Direction Relationship

My early experience illustrates some general principles that continue to inform my practice of spiritual direction both as director and directee, in one-to-one settings and in groups.

The spiritual direction relationship begins with an *invitation from God to be together*. It is surrounded by prayer and dominated by prayer. This prayer includes the prayer of the persons involved for one another.

Normally *one person serves as a director*, a person who looks with the directee for the direction of the Spirit, the vectors of love, in the directee's life. Even when people serve as directors for each other (as sometimes happens in one-to-one direction and usually in group direction) the intent of spiritual direction is best preserved if the roles of director and directee are well defined during any given session. This definition of roles helps protect the time committed for specific attention to each person's spiritual journey.

The directee assumes responsibility for his or her life with God. This means that those coming for direction are trying to be serious about intentional prayer and reflection on the God-currents in their prayer and in everyday lives, in whatever ways are authentic for them. This prayer and reflection usually provide the content for the meetings. In an atmosphere of prayer the director may question, challenge, and make suggestions as seems called for but ultimately whatever insights are uncovered or courses of action emerge must be owned by the directee. Both director and directee hope to be open to the surprising gifts of God's Spirit not only in their reflection on the past together but also in those "Aha's" seemingly unrelated to any content shared.

Although the focus may be on one of the persons in the relationship, it is very obvious that *God is gifting each person* through the presence of the other. It is as though the two are moved into a deeper place of knowing and loving together. This became very clear to me recently when I was with a woman in direction. She said to me, "You know, your questions always make me go deeper." I realized that what happens for me when I am with her is that as she speaks from the place of her authenticity, she draws me to another level of authenticity in myself. I respond from that place which then takes her to another level.[4]

Director and directee agree to pray for one another outside of meeting times. Their time together begins with prayer and is frequently punctuated with periods of silence. This silence is meant to be more than an absence of words. Ideally it is a choice for spaciousness in which director and directee can hear God's prayer for them, the "still small voice"[5] that may have become muted in the whirlwind of their words.

Ramana Maharshi, a Hindu sage, said, "If the guru keeps silence, there is between him and his disciple a communion and communication on a level much deeper than that of normal consciousness." In this silence director and directee can return together to their original intent and reclaim their desire for God. In this silence, they consciously seek an openness to the Holy Spirit who is the Real Director.[6]

Intercessory Prayer as Foundational to Spiritual Direction

This prayerful listening both fosters and reflects the attitude of intercessory prayer spoken of earlier as an availability to God for what is called for in the moment. In this stance of humility, directors gradually realize that they are not responsible for the spiritual life of another. Nor do they presume to know another's truth or what might be in the other's best interest. Rather there is a deep trust in the caring love of God which has been acting for the person long before these meetings and is active now in this moment. This trust frees directors to allow their skills, their experience and knowledge of the spiritual life, their knowledge and experience of the directee, all of their gifts and expertise, and their concern about the lack thereof, to be at the service of God's caring love.

Directees also come to an awareness of God's caring love as the foundation of their spiritual lives. Spiritual direction progressively becomes a means of asking directors to be present in that Love with them, supporting them in prayer. They are asking the directors also to lend an ear to their listening to God and to voice what they hear as directees pray, "God, give us Your perspective on what has been happening. How have You been present? How have You been addressing me through my thoughts, my feelings, my work, my relationships? What have you been trying to teach me about You? About me? What is Your prayer for me now? What do You want for me?"

This attitude of intercessory prayer, the willingness to enter into the prayer of God in us as God would have us care for ourselves, another, is the guiding principle for the deliberation of persons who are considering the possibility of being in direction together. The awareness of the presence or absence of this intercessory prayer can also alert the persons of the rightness of continuing together or terminating. I find that often when God is inviting me into God's caring love for another through spiritual direction there is a consciousness of carrying the other in my heart. At times other than those when I deliberately set out to pray for directees, I find myself praying for them. If there is little evidence that this is happening, it *may* be a sign that God is moving me out of the direction relationship.

Assessing the Appropriateness of the Relationship

Other things also need to be considered in continuing the direction relationship. It is well to reflect periodically on how things are going during the time of direction. This reflection on the time together is not meant to be an evaluation of what has been accomplished during the time together. In fact, since most sessions will usually not have a specific goal, there may be nothing that can be measured, nothing tangible to claim. If the persons involved are outcome-oriented, by pushing to make something happen they may miss God's invitation to be gently present, maybe seeming to waste time with God.

"Wasting time with God together"—being with God without specific agenda—is another way that I have come to describe prayerfulness. The time of reflection on the sessions offers the opportunity to pray over one's desire for prayerfulness during the sessions as well as one's freedom for that prayerfulness. In this reflection, director and directee pray for a sense of God's perspective on how things have been going. Individually and together they might reflect on such questions as: Are we still doing what we had hoped to do when we began this relationship? Is that still appropriate? What has changed in our relationship? What change is called for? Do we seem to be coming to a deeper sense of God together, or are we sidetracked by the dynamics of our relationship?

After years of being together, my first director said to me, "I think we should stop meeting for spiritual direction. I would like to be a friend, but I find that I am no longer free enough to listen with you for what God may be doing in your life. When you talk about your pain, I want to go out and rescue you from the people who are causing you that pain." I protested that this hadn't gotten in the way for me, but he knew it had for him. He said he had come to care too much for me emotionally to be of real assistance in discernment. He was no longer able to be freely present to God's caring love for me.

Since that time I have had several different directors. Each of them seemed right for a time, but I also recognized when it was time to move on. I chose one because it seemed that we had something in common in our spiritual journeys. While that was true, it proved not helpful to me after a while. Often we moved into spiritual conversations which were wonderful and inspiring, but such conversations took the focus off God's presence in my life. While I welcomed this at times, I realized that it was really not assisting my discernment. I was not free to be myself, to claim the uniqueness of God's way of dealing with me within our conversations.

I chose another director for precisely the opposite reason: I wanted someone very different from me. This person was married and of a denomination different from mine. Despite these seeming differences, and despite the fact that this person did not always understand my theological orientation, discernment could happen. He was able to respect my unique relationship with God and to help me explore the implications of that relationship in my life. Sometimes when I was feeling uncomfortable with my relationship with God, I would attempt to divert our attention by posing some theological issue. Always he brought me back to the point of our being together: "What does this have to say to you about God? What does God have to say to you about this?"

Eventually I came to realize that it didn't matter if my director was a man or woman, married, single or vowed religious, a person of the same or different denomination. It also didn't matter if direction happened within the context of a one-to-one relationship or in a group setting. What mattered was that those involved were responding to an invitation from God to be together and that we trusted God's presence in our response to this invitation more than we trusted ourselves.

This is what it takes for authentic spiritual direction to happen. Wherever people are willing to accept the responsibility of staying in God's presence on behalf of others with the intention of assisting those persons in their ongoing discernment, authentic spiritual direction can happen. It can happen as surely in group settings as in one-to-one settings.

Chapter 3

Discernment and Spiritual Direction

"It is because one antelope will blow the dust from the other's eye that the two antelopes walk together."

African Proverb[1]

Overview of Discernment

This African proverb is describing, I think, the role of spiritual directors in our discernment. In spiritual direction, another person or a group sits with us in the caring love of God, helping us notice how this caring love has been present for us. Through questioning, challenging, or simply being present in prayer, the other blows the dust from our eyes so that we might come to recognize the leading of God's Spirit within us. Occasionally others may clarify our vision by offering their insights for our consideration but ultimately we must claim whatever truth we see as well as its implications for our lives.

Seeing what God gives us to see is often referred to as discernment which means literally to perceive clearly, to judge accurately. To discern is to sift through the illusory. It is to come to discover what is real.

Discernment is referred to in different ways by many religious traditions.

The Sioux Native American tradition speaks of the "Eye of the Great Spirit" enlightening our hearts so that we might "see everything" and through this vision help our neighbor.[2]

In Hindu literature we read, "Braham is in all. He is action,

24

knowledge, goodness supreme. To know him, hidden in the lotus of the heart, is to untie the knot of ignorance."[3]

There is a story told in Buddhism about a monk who sought instruction from a great patriarch. When the patriarch had finished speaking, the monk asked, "Besides the secret words and secret meaning you have just now revealed to me, is there anything else, deeper still?" The patriarch replied, "What I have just told you is no secret at all. When you look into your true self, whatever is deeper is found right there."[4]

Christian Scriptures remind us, "It is the mysterious wisdom... the wisdom that was hidden, which God...has given through revelation of the Spirit, for the Spirit explores the depths of everything, even the depths of God."[5]

In the yogic traditions the word for discernment is "viveka" which means "to sense the will of God in the moment."[6]

Saint Ignatius of Loyola, out of reflection on his experience, wrote a classical treatise on discernment. There he speaks of the end of discernment as "finding God in all things" in order that we might love and serve God in all. He speaks of prayer as the means of discernment. For Saint Ignatius and others who write about discernment, discernment happens in the sure knowledge that God loves us, continuously guides us in love, and invites us to participate in love by loving others.[7]

Somehow, as the work of Saint Ignatius and others has come down to us through the years, we have separated the will of God from God, and discernment has come to mean a search for God's will which we must find in a game of hide-and-seek. We often equate discernment with a skill which we must master rather than the gift of God's love which guides us home to Love.

Prayer as the Atmosphere of Discernment

It is in the loving presence of God that we come to be discerning. Prayer, then, is the starting place of discernment as well as the atmosphere in which it happens. Prayer for our part is our way of honoring our relationship with God. It fine-tunes the heart to the prayer of God in us, God's desire for us. Gradually we come to live out of that desire in all of life. Attachments are more easily recognized and we are freed for more authentic choices that are congruent with our desire. Discernment, then, must always include prayer, and intentional prayer must become the subject of our discernment from time to time.

I remember the first time someone asked me about my prayer, how it fit with my experience of God. At first I had no answer. Then I was brought back to a childhood memory which shed light on my attitude toward prayer. When I was a child my mother would dress me and my two sisters in our best velvet dresses with their scratchy crinoline petticoats to go visit our two maiden cousins. We were reminded that we meant a great deal to them and that they really wanted us to come. But we were also told that they did not often have children visiting them so we should be on our best behavior. We should sit quietly on the sofa and only speak when spoken to, always being polite. If they asked us what refreshments we would like we should say, "Oh, whatever you would like." (What they liked usually consisted of grapefruit juice and strawberry ice cream when what I wanted was coke and potato chips.)

I had no doubt that these two women really loved us. I even grew to appreciate them. But I never liked to visit them. Even as an adult I fell into old patterns of behavior with them. I always wanted to please them, tried to figure out what would make them happy.

I realize that my image of God somehow had become linked with my image of these two cousins. My behavior toward God in prayer, even as an adult, was much like my behavior toward them. I was still sitting quietly on God's sofa in my scratchy crinoline, trying not to move. I was still being polite with God. I never asked for anything. I always said, "Whatever you would like, God, just tell me, just give me." I had learned from my cousins that if I wanted something God must not want it and what God wanted would be terrible.

I had come to know something different about God in my experience, however. My experience told me that God delighted to be with me whether I was dressed in my party finery or in my tattered jeans, whether I was sitting quietly on a sofa or playing

Frisbee on the beach. God just wanted to be with me, sharing my dreams and my desires. When God asked me what I wanted, God meant it. I could give a straight answer.

Once I realized that my image of God no longer matched my experience although I was still praying out of that image, I was stymied. I didn't know where to go from there. Then my director asked, "How would you like to pray? How would you like to be with God? How would you like God to be with you? Can you talk with God about it?"

I did talk with God about it and my prayer changed. I was no longer bound to a particular form. I could sit quietly or sing or simply take a walk and that was my prayer. I chose to be with God this way, and most times I trusted that this was prayer. But sometimes I doubted the rightness of my prayer, wondering if I was really praying or just deluding myself. At such times I tried to return to the more formal kind of prayer I had known. But I couldn't do it for long; it no longer fit.

From this experience, I realized that I could no longer take my prayer for granted. Periodically there would need to be discernment concerning this intentional prayer. I would need to notice if my prayer continued to honor and reflect God's presence in my life. I knew I would need help with this. I also knew that this discernment should be included in the ongoing conversations of all spiritual direction.

Prayer as the Subject of Discernment

Discernment on prayer is really prayer about our prayer. In this prayer we open ourselves to God's gaze, looking with God at God's desire for us, our desire for God, noticing how our prayer reflects these desires. Gradually, almost imperceptibly, our prayer becomes an expression of what we have come to know about God and ourselves through this looking.

Frequently a growing discontent or dis-ease with prayer suggests the need for discernment. For some, familiar, previously dependable methods of prayer just aren't working anymore; God is not present in the once familiar ways. For others, there has been a gradual awakening to God that moves them into unfamiliar terrain; the time of spiritual direction becomes important to explore this terrain. Then there are those for whom prayer seemed adequate until they heard someone else speaking about prayer or read a book that described prayer in rather esoteric terms. Since then they have wondered if they had been confused about what they have understood and practiced regarding prayer.

Sometimes when looking at our prayer, we want to move too quickly from the simple awareness of an experience to an interpretation of it. As we notice our heart's stirrings, or a new way of experiencing ourselves in relation to God, we might try to decipher the meaning of the experience for our lives or grasp after an appropriate response. A person might tell a director, "When I was praying last month I used the passage in Isaiah that talks about the Spirit of the Lord being upon me. I felt such peace and strength. I thought, 'Surely God has a special mission in mind for me. I need to discover what that mission is.' I asked God about it but I heard nothing. The next week a job offer came to me. It really seemed challenging and exciting. I thought it was related to my prayer over the Isaiah passage, that God was now telling me what it meant for me, but when I went for an interview, nothing about the job seemed right. Now I am afraid to trust anything about my prayer. I'm not sure I am even praying."

There can be a graced edge to such mistrust. Sometimes it carries God's gentle invitation to go beyond our limits to a new level of intimacy, a place of limitless love. We may experience reluctance, fear, or sadness at the loss of the familiar and doubt our very desire for God because of these feelings. Yet we sense a rightness about what is going on in our prayer, though we cannot explain why. There may be a willingness to let go of some of our need to know the implications of our prayer, trusting God's presence, God's anointing in the present moment. The felt experience of God may no longer be so important to us. Our attachment to a specific time and place for prayer may be replaced, almost imperceptibly, by a prayerfulness in all of life.

A prayer of deep humility and trust may shape itself in our

hearts: "God, I don't know what's going on, why things have changed. If this is Your grace at work in me, I want it; if You want something different, please let me know what it is. Most of all, just let me be with You."

When another person can enter this prayerful stance with us, then together we might see what we were unable to see alone. Perhaps the need for something different is indicated. Perhaps there is a form that can more authentically express our desire right now. Perhaps there is a simple formless presence that might divest us of hidden expectations about prayer. We might find that spiritual direction helps to sustain us as we wait for God. In this faithful waiting, mistrust of ourselves may give way to a deepening trust of God's Spirit at work in us. We might even begin to trust God's leading in our response to the question we put to ourselves: "How would I really like to pray? How would I like to be with God?"

There are times, however, when mistrust deflects our heart's attention. Our gaze shifts from God and a desire for God to a narrow preoccupation with self: "I should know more. I should be able to pray this way. I should be able to bypass these feelings and settle into prayer. I can't be myself with God; nothing about myself is quite good enough for prayer." Typically, then, we try to master prayer, forgetting that it has more to do with our wanting God and God's wanting us than any skill we might acquire. In our spiritual direction we might be helped to recall times when prayer arose quite spontaneously in our hearts. Then we might remember what we already know, that prayer is God's initiative, that God indeed has already taken that initiative in our hearts and our hearts have responded. Even though there may be some practices that can help us cut through our images of ourselves as praying persons, no practice can ever make the prayer happen.

In *The Screwtape Letters*, C.S. Lewis presents wise and witty guidance concerning discernment in prayer, using a series of letters from Screwtape, a senior devil, to his nephew, Wormwood. After presenting Wormwood with many ploys of distraction for the praying person, Screwtape says to Wormwood, "You will be helped by the fact that humans themselves do not desire prayer as much as they suppose. There is such a thing as getting what they bargained for." He then balances this with the admonition, "But, of course the Enemy will not meantime be idle. Whenever there is prayer, there is danger of God's own immediate action."[8]

We may never clearly discern all the intricacies of our prayer, even with the most gifted of spiritual directors. Despite all our fervor we may never be able to depend on our desire. But God's prayer in us is constant, as is God's love. Our hearts can rest in God's loving prayer. Here is the grace of it all, the hope of our spiritual lives.

Discernment and Decision Making

Just as we can trust God's loving prayer for us in our prayer, so too we can trust that prayer for us in all of life, including the decisions we must make. As we join the prayer of God within us, our defenses and our images of ourselves are gradually chipped away; we begin to know ourselves for who we are in God— beings who are loved very much, who are invited to become who we really are, beings in love. From that place of core identity we want to make decisions compatible with who we are. We have tasted the fruit of love in our own lives; we want to love others as we are loved. Sometimes, though, we forget what we have learned from love. We revert to asking questions like: "How can I be sure that I am doing God's will? How do I know that what I discern is really what God wants and not just what I want? How can I be sure I will make the right decision?" We may then look for processes that will guarantee the rightness of our decisions.

There is no human process that can protect us from mistakes and failures. We will never really be sure of the right course of action. As long as we are human and dealing with other human beings we will be subject to uncertainty and ambiguity in our motives. We can, however, open ourselves to God in the uncertainty, in the ambiguity, and allow the compulsion for rightness to be transformed into an openness to responsible love.

In the process of transformation, the gradual change that occurs within us through our cooperation with God's gracious action, we often vacillate between a trust in the sure guidance of Love that is God's will within us, and the feverish pursuit of God's will as though it were something outside us that we are left on our own to discover. In the stance of trust we can wait for Love to unfold. We can ask of ourselves with God, "What do I want? What do I really want?" and believe that in that answer Love will begin to show itself. In this stance, discernment may be seen as something of a dance: "And they started to dance like old lovers who know and cherish each other's grace; and his arm never pushed or pulled her, and her eyes never left his face."[9] When discernment is seen in this way we look to a spiritual director to challenge us to keep our eyes on God and to help us uncover the drivenness of our unfreedoms that keep us from enjoying the dance.

In the stance of feverish pursuit, discernment becomes a game of hide-and-seek where we need all the help we can get to discover what has been hidden by God in the maze of life outside us. In this case we seek a spiritual director to help us be sure we have looked in all the nooks and crannies where God's will might be hidden or we ask a spiritual director to tell us where it is hidden. A spiritual director might, out of a need to be helpful, get trapped into giving us answers or working hard to help us find them, as I often did.

There was a time when knowing what God wanted, responding rightly to love, was very important to me. It was as though I could confirm my loving by my knowing. If I had the "right" loving response, then I would be loving. And, "If I am truly loving, then I will have the right loving response, to prayer, to life, to friends, to God." When others asked what God might want in a given situation, I was more than eager to help them find an answer. I tried to ask the right questions, to examine thoroughly every possibility of what God might want, all for the sake of love. Often, though, we lost sight of love. The passion for knowing eclipsed the love and there was little room for trust.

I was recently reminded of my earlier propensity for knowing by a woman whom I had been seeing for about ten years. We had been talking together for nearly an hour during a time of spiritual direction. Several times she had asked the same question, "Rose

Mary, what do you think? Is this what God wants?" Each time I answered her question with other questions, not unlike those of my former director: "What do you think? Why is it so important to be sure? Are you able to be with God in your questions? What have you said to God about it? What do you think would happen if you just tried out this decision before you were clear about what God wanted?"

Consistently her responses revealed her primary concern, her love of God and her desire to do the loving thing. She was afraid that her choice was coming only from a place of selfishness, not from God. When after nearly an hour I offered no direct answer to her question she blurted out her frustration: "You used to tell me, Rose Mary! You used to be able to tell me whether something was of God!"

I knew she was right. I had often responded to such a need for knowing. This time, however, I had no answer. After a long silence I managed to be truthful: "I just don't know anymore. The more I listen to myself and others the less certain I am of what God wants in a given situation. Sometimes I don't have a clue about what's really going on in me or where something is coming from. All I know is that I have come to trust God more in my unknowing than I did in my knowing. I am not always comfortable in this place, but it's the only place I can be."

Deep inside, I was grateful for the place of unknowing. I wanted this woman to be there also. But that had to be God's work. The best I could do was risk not having an answer. It seemed God's only recourse in getting me there was to divest my mind of images and to complicate my knowing. There is nothing left then but to trust and, in the theology of Julian of Norwich, to act as though I believe in the goodness of God.[10]

It is true that our desire to love needs illumination to see clearly the objects of choice. In seeking the Reality of Love we are faced with our myopia and our inability to judge accurately even what we do see. Often a spiritual director can widen our scope of vision and elucidate the facts. A spiritual director also may help us uncover the non-negotiables, those areas of our lives which we withhold from God, that keep us looking in the wrong places.

We can never know all there is of any given circumstance. And the truth often transcends the obvious. There comes a time when we are invited into simple faith as we make decisions, trusting God to transform the ambiguity of our hearts with the fire of love and to be with us in and through the uncertainty. We have done what we can. Our task is to live into the decision, seeking (when available) the support of others who share our desire for God. Gradually we come to live in a place of love and allow that love to lead. God's loving prayer in us becomes the testing place of discernment. Through the lens of that loving prayer we view our choices and come to recognize our authenticity.

The Habit of Discernment

Perhaps another way of saying this is that ultimately we realize that God is in love with us. We fall in love with God. As a Roman Catholic priest once wrote:

Nothing is more practical than finding God, i.e. than falling in love in a quite absolute, final way.

What you are in love with, what seizes your imagination, will affect everything. It will decide what will get you out of bed in the morning, what you do with your evenings, how you spend your weekends, what you read, whom you know, what breaks your heart, what amazes you with joy and gratitude. Fall in love, stay in love—and it will decide everything.[11]

When we are in love, we dwell in the place of love which Thomas Kelly names the "holy abyss, where the Eternal dwells at the base of our being." He speaks of the need to "center down" and "live in that holy Silence which is dearer than life," taking all of our life, including our decisions, into that place with us. He is describing here the habitual attitude of discernment that I referred to earlier as prayerfulness. This discerning attitude is a way of gradually coming to live out of our desire for God in all of life.[12]

Spiritual direction nourishes the habitual attitude of discernment. In spiritual direction those involved seek to be present to God together, dwelling in that holy Silence of Love where whatever has clouded our vision gradually is burned away. We are offered new facets of truth that help us see what we could not see alone.

Sometimes we can see more clearly with the assistance of a single other person. At other times, it is the prayerful presence of a group that helps us to stay in the flame of our love. In group spiritual direction, as in one-to-one spiritual direction, people are present together in the Mystery of Love explicitly to assist one another in discernment. The group becomes a spiritual director for each person in the group. Through the interceding presence of the group, the dust is blown from our eyes. We see more clearly the presence of God in our lives.

Chapter 4

The Practice of
Group Spiritual Direction

"Unless we are grounded in Mystery—unless we experience both ourselves and others as co-participants in Mystery—we find it almost impossible to live in compassionate love of one another for any length of time. Unless we have 'new eyes' that can see the others contemplatively, it is easy to miss the many-splendored thing that is our life together."

Carolyn Gratton[1]

Group spiritual direction is grounded in Mystery. We use a very simple process which honors and supports this grounding: silence, the sharing of a participant, silence, response from the group, silence. We repeat this process until all individuals have had time for their sharing and response from the group. We add a few minutes at the end to reflect on our time together. Sometimes, if it seems that we have lost sight of the Mystery or our reason for being together, we return to silence in the midst of our response to an individual.

Prayerful silence nurtures discernment in group spiritual direction, just as it does in one-to-one spiritual direction. However, discernment occurs differently in the two direction settings. In one-to-one spiritual direction, discernment happens primarily through our willingness to invite another into our discernment and our attempts to articulate the God-noticings in our lives. In group spiritual direction, although there is usually less time for attention to individuals, people often become aware of God's ways in their hearts as they hear how God seems to be present for others and as they become conscious of God's presence with them as a group. God breaks open the tiny vessels they each have built to contain God. They come to expect God in surprising places in their lives and the lives of others.

In group spiritual direction people learn to listen to God's Spirit at work in them for others in the group. As they take the sharing of others into the resting place of shared silence they seek to respond to what has been disclosed out of that prayerful place. Thus there is a collective wisdom available for each person. Whereas in one-to-one direction there is a single other person to lend vision to the directee, a group affords the possibility of many faces of truth being uncovered in any given situation. Persons are challenged to take the words of others into the place of Mystery where they can claim what is real for them.

As a spiritual director, I find that once a group has coalesced, prayerfulness comes much more easily for me in the group setting than in one-to-one direction. In one-to-one direction I can get caught in my "role," thinking that I must have insightful questions to offer the person. In group spiritual direction, I can rest more easily into God's presence in the community and trust God to communicate in God's timing.

Three conditions are essential to the life of the group. Members must agree to commit themselves to 1) an honest relationship with God; 2) wholehearted participation in the group process through prayerful listening and response; and 3) opening their spiritual journeys to the consideration of others.

Although these conditions, of themselves, do not guarantee the effectiveness of group spiritual direction, they do foster and reflect the willingness needed to engage in such a process. The depth of sharing necessary in group spiritual direction demands a level of trust not often found in other types of groups. This trust is not dependent upon similar personalities, mutual interests or common experiences; rather it is grounded in a trust of God's desire for each participant individually as well as the group as a whole.

An individual in a short-term group spiritual direction experience wrote to me of her initial reaction:

In my group was a man who had aroused in me a number of judgments. I had almost prayed that I wouldn't have to be with this person in a group. When I found we were together, I felt every button being pushed and was quite desperate about surviving our sessions. Feeling at the mercy of my mind and emotions, and seeing no escape, I tried to recall our purpose for being together—to pray for one another.

I began to pray, seeing myself sitting in a room with Christ. There were no words. We just sat together as I experienced Christ's presence very intimately. Then He looked at me and asked, "Shall we invite him to join us now?" My response was, "Yes," and I meant it. In the following sessions I moved to a place of empathy, even affection. I began to trust the experience that brought us together and I was transformed by the process of prayer.

What draws people to spiritual direction is a reciprocity of desire. Having been touched by God's desire, they want to make their desire for God the determining factor of all of their choices, and they recognize that they need some help to do this. This shared desire is the group's cohesion. People share a commitment to be there for each other in their desire for God. In the group they make their shared desire explicit. They hold one another in the prayer of their desire.

Faithful Looking

When asked by a friend how she prayed for her, Julian of Norwich responded, "I look at God, I look at you, and I keep on looking at God."[2] Put simply, the group's task is to keep on looking at God for each person in the group. People know this faithful looking is why they are together and they really want that for themselves and for the group. Yet they may unintentionally collude to avoid it. They may become busy about many things besides spiritual direction. They need a process that will help them do what they came to the group to do.

The process described here is only one of many that can facilitate spiritual direction for individuals within a group setting. It is a process that I and others who work with me at the Shalem Institute have come to trust. Having evolved over the years, it seems to express our sense of what is important about spiritual direction and to foster what we hope will happen during group meetings.

Overview of the Process

I have designed this process for use in a setting of four or five groups that meet simultaneously in separate rooms. Each group contains three or four participants who may not know one another before they come to the group. Each group has a facilitator who functions as time-keeper and who at least initially protects the climate of prayerful listening for the group. Facilitators need not be experienced spiritual directors. It is essential, however, that they appreciate the process they will facilitate. Usually the facilitators have another place for their own spiritual direction and they make this clear to the group. In the interest of time, they are not a directee in the group, but they do share fully in the rest of the process.

It is important to establish the groups in their common purpose. Therefore we begin each year with a full day during which we describe what our time together will be. We also introduce faith sharing. In order to keep the momentum of the opening day's sharing, the first few meetings are closely spaced, usually at approximately two week intervals. After that, groups meet approximately every four weeks for eight months. At the end of this time there is a two-month break. Individuals may choose to continue together, join a different group, or discontinue group spiritual direction. This process for ongoing group direction can be adapted for short-term use in retreat settings. It can be used also by groups such as parish staffs who want to reflect on the grace inherent in their working together. Support groups may find it helpful in moving to a deeper level of sharing. Such groups might choose an outside facilitator to assist them, at least initially, or may simply rotate the convening of the group.

A woman in the Stephen Ministry of one-to-one care in time of need, said of her experience of meetings with other Stephen ministers:

> After meeting for months, providing support and supervision in our ministry, we decided to move into group spiritual direction together. Our response was favorable. We felt less responsible for problem solving, less prone to offer suggestions. The periods of prayer helped us to focus on our being care givers, not cure givers, as our training teaches. As we listened prayerfully to one another, there was less reaching for the right words, perfect response, the ideal suggestion. We felt more a oneness in our ministry, aware of the presence of the Holy Spirit in our work, guided by this Presence and supported by the prayer of one another.

Opening Day

A. OVERVIEW OF COMPONENTS

We begin with five or six hours, usually on a Saturday, in which we hope to lay a foundation for what is going to be happening through the year, especially the practice of prayerful listening and speaking which is essential to group spiritual direction. In designing the day we consider such variables as the familiarity of participants with contemplative prayer, silence, and spiritual direction, as well as differences in denomination and/or theology, and the acquaintance of participants with one another.

Participants who do not know one another may need informal opportunities to hear some human specifics of the lives of other participants, so that they can begin to feel naturally comfortable with one another. On the other hand, if people know one another from other settings, they may need more formal time in which to establish the way of being together which undergirds group spiritual direction. When people come from different denominational or theological backgrounds, they need time to begin to hear through the seeming diversity to common understandings. People from similar backgrounds may assume a common understanding in the language they use, though, in fact, the experiences underneath the language may be very different. These people need to explore the differences that exist among them. Whether or not participants have known each other before, there must be time for them to begin to claim and articulate their faith experience and to hear the words others use to describe their experience.

Within the opening day we allow forty-five minutes for personal prayer followed by one hour for small group sharing, forty-five minutes for lunch, and forty-five minutes for a "real play" of group spiritual direction—an actual time of spiritual direction for one person with others who have been in group spiritual direction being the spiritual directors. We follow this with a discussion of the process in small groups. We divide the remaining time among other components depending upon the size and needs of the group.

B. DETAILED DESCRIPTION OF THE OPENING DAY

1. Introduction

We begin with a brief period of silent prayer to gather our hearts consciously into the Mystery of Love. We ask people to introduce themselves, sharing why they have come to the group. We acknowledge what we have heard in silent prayer.

2. Sharing of Assumptions

• Concerning Our Reason for Being Together

We talk about our reason for being together as flowing from a shared desire for God and a recognition of the need to have others accompany us as the journey of that desire unfolds. We are committed to supporting the others in that journey.

• Concerning the Community of Each Small Group

We share our assumptions concerning small groups to reinforce their purpose—group spiritual direction. We remind participants and ourselves as facilitators that this community is not an end in itself, nor is it designed to meet a variety of needs within or outside the group. The intention of this community is to support our relationship with God. We set parameters around the responsibilities of participants toward one another, namely prayer for one another and full participation in each meeting. There are no obligations outside the time of the meetings other than that of prayer for one another.

• Concerning the Role of Silence Within the Process

Silence is an important element of the group's time. In talking about it, we try to be sensitive to other experiences people have had with silence. Some things people have said are:

"I'm never very comfortable with silence. I tend to associate it with my mother's way of expressing disapproval."

"In my Afro-American cultural tradition, if the Spirit of God is in you there should be some visual sign or verbal response. Periods of silence are experienced as the departing of the anointing of the Spirit. Once when I paused at the beginning of my sermon, people began to pray aloud that God would give me some words to say."

"I'm not a good conversationalist. I'm always glad to be in a group where people are not too talkative. It gives me a chance to think of what to say."

"I hate it when people are silent. I always think they are afraid to speak their minds. I'd rather have disagreements out in the open."

"I'm an extrovert and silence is just not natural for me. It's too inhibiting."

After acknowledging possible difficulties, we speak of silence as a way of consciously making space for God together. We tell people that since we believe we are together only to listen to God for and with one another, we surround and punctuate our time with prayerful silences. We encourage people to risk speaking out of the silence what they sense is being given for another but not to feel compelled to speak. Whatever words we have for one another need to come from a place of prayerful listening. It is to prayerful listening that we must return.

It may happen that no words are spoken in response to a person's sharing. At times we may realize that we are too close to what the presenter has talked about to be prayerful in our response. At other times, we may not understand what the presenter is saying although we sense it is very important to the person. We may offer our silent support. Still at other times we may be profoundly touched through the sharing of another and silently celebrate God's presence with us.

The group's prayerful presence together does not guarantee that everything that is spoken in the group comes directly from God. It simply gives expression to a willingness to be present to God for one another. The fruitfulness of the group's time together can't be measured in terms of words spoken, insights gained, or truth uncovered, but rather in terms of a growing receptivity to God, as individuals and as a group.

• Concerning the Role of the Facilitator

In introducing the role of the facilitator, we stress the fundamental responsibility of each group for its process. We try to convey that the facilitators are facilitators simply because they have had some experience in the process and are willing to make their experience available to the group, not because their spirituality is superior to that of others in the group or because they have more wisdom. Facilitators will help the groups get started by doing some modeling of the process and by intervening when a group seems to get deflected from its purpose. While they will be conveners and time keepers for groups throughout the year, soon they will challenge participants to assume responsibility for the process of the group. We also tell participants that facilitators meet before each session for prayer and that they meet after the session as well, to review the flow of the meeting. We emphasize that facilitators hold in confidence the content of what is shared in the group and expect that everyone else will observe that same confidentiality.

3. Time of Personal Prayer and Reflection

After this introductory discussion, we move into some time of intentional prayer and reflection, encouraging people to be present to God in whatever way is most fitting for them. We suggest that during part of this time people reflect on who God is for them right now, how they perceive God to be present in their lives and what it is they call prayer.

It is difficult to encourage this reflection so early in the process without seeming to be intrusive or to give the impression that one has expectations of the way things "should" be between the person and God. Even to ask people how they experience God can suggest that they "should" have some tangible experience of God. We say clearly that there are no "should's" about prayer, no right or wrong ways to pray.

Since one's faith experience becomes the backdrop for all discernment that will happen in the groups, the plunge into our faith experience needs to be taken and spoken of early on. We tentatively suggest that for at least part of the forty-five minutes of silence people pray over such questions as: "Who is God for me? What has been going on between God and me? How is it that God seems to be relating to me? How am I relating to God? What does my being here have to do with the way God and I are together?" I give some Scripture quotes and other readings that I have found helpful in offering different images for that reflection.[3]

I suggest that people might want to look to nature for such images as well. Or there might be a word, a gesture, or some art work that can begin to articulate their faith experience to others. I ask that before people end the time of reflection they consider the questions: "Are there practices or people that support and honor my relationship with God? Are there practices or people that I would like to have support me in my relationship with God?"

4. Small Group Sharing Following the Time of Prayer

Following personal prayer the small groups meet with their

facilitators who talk briefly about the diversity that is present in every group and the need to listen through the words of another to the reality that is being expressed. Sometimes, in order to touch into this reality, it will be necessary to ask for a translation of words we do not understand. At other times, even when we can understand the words, we may not understand the experience because it is so foreign to our own. On the other hand, there may be a tendency to project our interpretation on the experience of another because it seems so similar to ours. Then we miss what the person or God has to say about the experiences.

In each instance, we can listen for the way the experience seems to be speaking of God to the other. More importantly, we can take the person's words to a place of prayer and open our confusion, our lack of understanding or our clarity to God. In doing so we express our willingness to trust God's presence for the person more than we trust our attempts to respond in a helpful way.

This initial time of sharing does not call for any response, nor is there time for discussion. It is simply an opportunity for participants and the facilitator to put a little of their sacred stories before the group. This sharing is different from the time of interaction of the ongoing meetings. It helps members begin to speak and hear one another from a place of prayer and become familiar with the content of spiritual direction. It also removes a certain mystique from the facilitators since they share about their prayer during this time. We ask group members specifically to offer something of what came out of the preceding time of prayer about their life with God, their prayer, how this relates to their coming to the group, and what kind of practices they have to support their spiritual life right now. We ask people to refrain from recounting past events of their lives unless these have come alive in some fresh way during their prayer, shedding light on their current, lived reality with God.

An example of what people might share during this time is:

Last month when I was walking to work I saw a homeless person sleeping on the street. She was there every day, and every day I tried to avoid looking at her. Then I started to leave a bag of food for her. Finally one day I stopped and took a good look at her. I realized she had something to say to me about myself. I feel so restless and so homeless. I pray every day for about ten minutes with Scripture. One day I opened to the verse where Jesus said, "Make your home in me." I felt that He was talking directly to me, but I don't know what that means or what to do about it. I don't have many places where I can talk about this sort of thing. I thought maybe this group could help me look at it.

After everyone has shared, there is time to talk about hopes and fears in relation to group spiritual direction. We find that giving people an opportunity to voice their fears in the beginning helps them realize that they are not alone in their apprehensions. Also, hearing the hopes of others allows facilitators to address unrealistic expectations.

Some typical things that people say during this time are:

"I want to be here and in the silence I felt good about it. But when I heard all of you, I became uncomfortable. I'm afraid I don't belong. I'm not very spiritual."

"I'm not very good at talking about myself. I'm afraid no one will understand me."

"I'm so glad for a group like this. I've been going it alone for so long. I need some company."

"I've been in one-to-one spiritual direction. Now I think I'm at a point where I might be helped more by hearing from other people about their spiritual journeys. I think this group will offer that."

"I want to get closer to God but I'm afraid. I don't know what God will ask of me."

Then we have a pot luck lunch together. In seeing the diversity of the group, group members often come away with a sense of belonging there, that there is no one kind of person who fits the description of being "spiritual." One participant in group spiritual direction at Shalem said of this experience: "After getting to know the people not in my small group, those people became for me concrete metaphors for the Body of Christ."

5. *Real Play and Follow-Up Discussion*

After lunch we gather again in the large group for a half-hour "real play" of a group session with facilitators and/or others who have previously participated in group spiritual direction forming the group. This is "real" to the extent that the directee presents something real from his or her spiritual life and the persons in the small group are there not just to model the process but to be real discerners with the directee. We ask participants to join in the process through their prayer, rather than being only observers.

After this session, the small groups reconvene to discuss and question what they have just observed. Where it has not seemed possible or advantageous to have the "real play," we have offered some reading about spiritual direction and discuss this in the small groups. Ordinarily, however, we give little direct attention to the theory of spiritual direction or the attitude of intercessory prayer which undergirds it. People become stuck in an intellectual discussion which can get in the way of their experiencing the reality under these words.

6. *Preparation for the Next Meeting*

Before their departure, I give the participants some questions to reflect on for our next gathering: "What are my names for God right now? What is my name for myself right now? What name might God have for me right now? What do these names have to say about my experience of God? How do I honor my experience with God?" I also encourage people to spend time in whatever intentional practice seems called for and to journal through music, words, or art as it seems appropriate. I am reluctant to say much about journaling because for some people it can become only an exercise in self-expression and for others a seemingly impossible burden. I do, however, suggest some reading on journaling for those who might be interested.[4]

Before our closing prayer we give out the dates for subsequent meetings and guidelines for our time together. The guidelines are as follows:

- Pray for others in the group between sessions in whatever way is right for you.

- Be consistent in whatever practice seems best to reflect and honor your unique relationship with God at this time, perhaps journaling about what you perceive, sense, or want concerning your attention to God and the way God seems to be dealing with you in all facets of your life. It could be helpful to notice things such as:

– your desire for God, your desire to desire God,
– the persons and circumstances that seem to draw you to God/connect you to God or to the meaning or the hope for your life,
– the way you sense God involved in your life, your resistance to God or areas where you shut out God, etc.

- Before coming to the group, spend time in prayer, reflecting on your prayer and your journaling since the last meeting, asking for a sense of what is to be shared. Allow for the possibility that something entirely different may show itself in the actual moment of your sharing.

- Come as early for the group as you wish but be prepared to start on time. Since some people might be using the room for prayer before you arrive, please enter the room in silence. (Those who want to socialize before the group begins can gather in another room.)

- During the time of small group sharing, continue in the prayerful presence begun in the large group, simply trying to be available to God in whatever way seems good for you. Try to be considerate of others in the group by confining your sharing to the allotted time, about twenty-five minutes per person, including what you share about yourself and the group's response. Look upon your time of sharing as a time for you to talk about your God-relationship as you are experiencing it in all areas of your life.

- Hold in reverence and confidence what you hear in the group.

- If you know you are going to be absent, let someone in the group know. If it is possible and you are comfortable doing so, send a note to group members, describing as well as you can what seemed to be going on between you and God during the past month. Perhaps you will be able only to talk about the way you would like people to be praying for you during the month. Hopefully this will ease your sharing at the next meeting; it may also give a focus for our time of prayer for you during the session and during the rest of the month.

NOTE: It is well to remember that these are only guidelines to assist us in our common purpose. The most important components of group spiritual direction are our willingness to be intentional about our spiritual journeys in whatever way is most authentic for us now, our prayerful presence/openness to God for one another, and our willingness to share our spiritual journeys with one another.

Subsequent Meetings

We meet again in ten days for two and a half hours. We gather first in a large group. At the beginning of this time we talk about the structure of this and subsequent meetings. It is difficult to know a large group of people on the level of prayer where discernment can take place. For the sake of time, sharing will be limited to the small group which will be constant through the year and where attention will be given to each person. The process we use in the group is structured in such a way as to make the best possible use of the time we have and to protect an atmosphere congruent with our intent.

A. LARGE GROUP GATHERING

The large group gathering generally lasts about twenty minutes, though we will be in the larger group longer for this meeting and the next. This opening time is an opportunity to gather our hearts into a common desire for God and to dedicate the evening for our world. Any business will be conducted at the beginning of this time. A facilitator may offer a brief reading from Scripture or elsewhere to ground us in God. The remainder of the time will be spent in silence so that people may pray as they feel led.

While it is expected that people have reflected on their life since the last meeting, some people may want to use the silence to pray about what they might bring to the group. This first evening I offer some questions to assist people in their reflection: "What are the times when I've found myself spontaneously being drawn to prayer, or to think about God or appreciate life? When have I noticed, at least after the fact, that I was very open to God? When have I found myself backing away from God? What is my prayer around this now? What do I want to say to God? What do I want to hear from God?"

A woman who has been in Shalem's group spiritual direction for several years said:

> I came to realize that this large group gathering is a crucial grounding for the following two hours in small groups and so requires something fundamental—loosening our hold on the ego so God will have the space to enter. As that happens for each of us, our time together creates the intimacy that is unique to being together in God without words. It gives the freedom to be authentic that is born in silence.... Without speaking we know we are united in a desire to be with God more and more deeply through each other. Together we sit and breathe, the most ancient form of prayer.[5]

B. SMALL GROUPS

After the silence we invite people to move into their small groups in silence. This silence helps people continue the prayerful listening which began in the large group. Facilitators then lead groups into the process that will be the same throughout all our small group times:

1. Continued silence (about 5 minutes) with an invitation for someone to begin sharing when he or she feels ready.

2. Sharing by one person (between ten and fifteen minutes).

If a presenter seems to be taking longer, the facilitator will remind the presenter that if he or she wants to hear from others in the group about the sharing it will be necessary to finish soon.

Often people find themselves talking about something entirely different from what they had planned to share. It seems that being in the intentional setting of the group helps people be aware of things that they are not aware of by themselves. We ask that whatever content the person is sharing be filtered through the lens of their ongoing relationship with God and that they try to share something of what their prayer has been like around the content. We suggest that persons try to avoid asking for information or solutions.

A person may find words difficult and simply say, "I'm not sure what is going on in me. Everything just seems dry—my relationships, my work, even my prayer. I'm sure I must be doing something wrong, but I don't know what. I've tried to ask God about it, but I don't get much feedback. Maybe you can help me."

Another might say, "This week I baby-sat with my six-week-old granddaughter. She is so beautiful! As I watched her, I became so appreciative of her, of life, of God. I realize how much beauty I've been missing by focusing on my problems. I know they are a part of my life too, but I want to see beyond them to what's really there. My prayer has been different this week. I haven't been asking God for things. I've just been grateful."

We ask that the group listen prayerfully through to the end of the person's sharing without interruption.

3. Silence (3 or 4 minutes). This silence is a time for making space for God, for allowing God to cut through the limits of our biases and our habitual ways of responding so that we can respond to the person from a place of prayer. In the beginning, this silence can be difficult, especially for people who are accustomed to spontaneous group dialogue. Eventually most

people come to appreciate it, however, and those who do not are at least willing to tolerate it for the sake of the group.

4. Response (about ten minutes, usually invited by the facilitator). As questions or comments come up they are offered to the presenter. At times there is such a sense of God being intimately in that moment that there may be no words. If the person has shared something very painful or very intriguing, the group may become very talkative, wanting to "fix things" for the person or simply being curious. The facilitator or someone else in the group may ask for silence to bring the group back to where they can listen to God together. Silence might also be suggested if it seems that participants are offering too many different ideas or images to the person. All of these might be appropriate but together they are too much for the person to deal with at a given time. Presenters should ask for silence if they feel they need it.

We encourage people to trust God's caring love present for the person in the silence and also in the words. We ask them to listen to the response of others and move with the flow of the group instead of holding onto a personal agenda for the presenter. At times it may seem that, for the sake of having time for all participants, the discussion with one person must be ended somewhat prematurely. It is helpful to remind the group that since the spiritual life is ongoing, there does not need to be closure in any one session. Also, our presence to the person is not meant to replace the person's presence to God which must continue as the person leaves the group.

5. Silence (about five minutes). During this time we suggest that people pray for the person who has just presented. The presenter may want to take some notes on what he or she has heard.

6. Repeat of the process, with a short break midway, until all members have presented

Here is an example of what might happen in a group once it becomes grounded in the process:

One person relates her difficulty in knowing what God is asking in her workplace where she feels the dis-ease of silent collaboration with unjust systems. She gives some examples of when she most often feels this dis-ease. The group is silent. Out of the silence emerges the question: "Have you asked what God might be asking?" Silence again and then the response, "I think I have avoided it because it might result in some risk-taking." The dialogue continues for a few minutes—no answers, only questions that help her probe her fear, her sense of God in the fear, and the call to justice in her life. One person begins talking about social justice issues. Another calls the group back to silence from which there can be discerning listening for the presenter. There are no more words to be spoken. They remain in silence a few minutes longer, praying for the presenter.

Another person talks about how things have changed for him in the past month. He says that things had become so busy at work that he couldn't think of much else or even pray. Then one Saturday, as he sat with his son, he was struck with this child's delight.

The little boy sat on the floor holding a piece of peeled apple, blabbering, singing, smiling as he chewed the apple. Things seemed so simple for him. He was with God and God was with him. As he gazed on his son, for a split second, he forgot his responsibilities. He was one with God.

He says that after that he felt lighter. Nothing seemed much of a burden. Prayer became easier because he didn't feel he had to do anything special. At work he could ease up a little and actually enjoy the people with whom he worked. He saw a beauty in his wife that he hadn't seen for a while. He was just very grateful for the change.

There is a long silence. No one has words to offer. People rest in their gratitude with him.

A third person says that prayer has been very difficult for her since her sister's death. There is a part of her that wants to pray and another part that wants to stay away from God. She can talk a little about her feelings concerning her sister's death with her support group but she can't bring her feelings to prayer.

Someone asks if she knows why she can't bring her

feelings to God. She responds that she's not sure if she trusts God right now. She thinks she is afraid. Then someone asks if it would help to try to pray about this now while the group is with her. She says that she is not ready to do this. Someone else asks what she wants from them. She says that she would like them to pray for her, that it is comforting to know that they are praying for her when she can't pray for herself. The group is silent; then someone prays aloud that she will know God's love for her in the midst of her pain. The group continues in silence.

7. Prayer for absent member (at least ten minutes). This can be inserted anywhere in the process, but preferably not at the end since it can easily be forgotten there.

In this prayer we honor the belief that the most important thing we can do for one another is to pray, and this prayer is not dependent on the physical presence of the other. Not only do we pray for the person who cannot be with us, we also ask members to pray for one another in whatever way is right for them outside the time of the group.

In the group described above, a fourth person was absent because of a death in his family. In a phone call to a woman in the group, he said that there would be some sticky family business to deal with. He asked her to tell the group that he wanted them to pray that he could let go of his sense of responsibility to make it all turn out right. The group prayed silently for him.

8. Reflection on the time together (about ten minutes, but longer until groups become familiar with the spirit of the process). This reflection is not meant to be an analysis of the time together or an effort to control future outcomes. Instead, it should be a gentle looking, noticing with God how the time together went, and an honest sharing around what is seen. The focus for this should be on the sense of prayerfulness within the group and within individuals. Whatever is addressed—silence, words, the human dynamics within the group—should be viewed in terms of prayerfulness, what has served it or gotten in its way.

I find the following questions helpful in facilitating this reflection:

How prayerful were we during this session? What was the quality of our silence? Our attention to God? What seemed to take us from attention to God?

How well did we stay focused on the spiritual life of each person, on the God relationship beneath the content of what people presented? Where did we get off course?

Were there places where we got "off track" (e.g. doing too much problem solving, being too analytical or philosophical, sharing our own experiences during another's time when it wasn't called for)?

When I was the directee, was I vulnerable, willing to share what seemed to be called for? Was I open to hearing what others had to say to me? Were there times when the words of another seemed to interrupt or get in the way of my discernment? Is there any feedback I need to give people about this?

As a listener for the others, where did my words or my silence seem to be coming from? A place of trust? A place of competition? My need to feel superior to others or appear learned? Am I willing simply to offer a question, an idea, or an image to a person for their consideration and then let go of it, or do I keep on pushing it? Do I listen to the questions of others, or do I hold onto my agenda for the person?

Is there any particular awareness or prayer that I take from our time together? Any particular way I would like the group to pray for me?

In the group described above, one person talked about his difficulty in staying in a prayerful place with the woman who talked about her fear of risk-taking. He felt the threat of risk-taking for himself and was uncomfortable with it. Others nodded in agreement. Then someone said, "I wonder if that's why we began to discuss social justice issues instead of staying with her."

Another talked about how hard it was not to try to rescue the woman who was in pain. She said she couldn't trust herself to respond. She just sat there praying, "God, take care of her."

Someone else said that he was almost glad that the fourth person wasn't present. He was afraid that he would have gotten hooked into giving advice. During the time of prayer for this man he finally realized that this is the most important thing they can do for one another.

People returned to silence. They prayed for one another. They celebrated the presence of love among them.

The Fruit of Dwelling in Love

When individuals take seriously the responsibility to stay grounded in the Mystery of Love, a group can give itself to the process of group spiritual direction. Then transformation occurs. The group emerges no longer merely a collection of people who want to be present to one another. Instead, members experience themselves as co-participants in the Mystery of Love. The group has become a spiritual community which celebrates the uniqueness of each individual's desire for God yet the commonality of that desire. People want to be present to God for one another in the fullness of that desire. The desire for God becomes the ground for their discernment. Together and alone they continue to examine choices for responsible love.

Chapter 5

Decisions: Participants, Groups, Facilitators

"When by grace we see something of God, then we are moved by the same grace to seek with great desire to see God for our greater joy. So I saw God and I sought God, I had God and I lacked God; and this is and should be our ordinary undertaking in this life as I see it."

Julian of Norwich[1]

Readiness for Group Spiritual Direction

Readiness for spiritual direction has something to do with the awareness of seeing God and seeking God, of having God and lacking God. It also has something to do with an awareness of how often we lose sight of God and even our desire for God. From this awareness we sense the rightness of involving another or others in this very ordinary undertaking of paying attention to God in our lives. Readiness for spiritual direction also implies an attitude of trustful openness out of which we will share the reflection on our prayer, our tending to God, and will listen to what rises in the silence and words of the direction time.

For group spiritual direction, this readiness for spiritual direction must be coupled with readiness for prayerful participation in a group process. It also suggests freedom for self-disclosure in a group, and an active seeking of the involvement of others in our discernment. With this readiness, we can allow other participants to be who they are with God and offer the fruit of our prayerful consideration of their words without the need to impose our belief system or experience on them.

In addition, there must be a basic trust in God's Spirit at work in ourselves and other participants as well as in the group process. This trust may come more naturally to some people than to others, depending upon theology and practice regarding the role of the Holy Spirit in the life of the individual and the community. Still, unless there is some expectation that God's Spirit can and will show itself in the gathered community in surprising ways, and unless there is an active commitment to seek the guidance of this Spirit for one another within the group interaction and also between meetings, group spiritual direction will be very ineffectual.

Participants

There is no foolproof method for ascertaining the readiness of persons for spiritual direction. In one-to-one direction this discernment, coupled with an attempt to sense the fitness between the two people involved, often takes place during the first few months of exploration, with either having the option to terminate. In group direction there are others who will be contracting with the person in this venture. It is important for the participants and leader to have the opportunity to explore the appropriateness of group direction for applicants and to arrive at as much clarity as possible before the first meeting.

Just as there is a right time for people to choose one-to-one spiritual direction, so there is a time when it may be appropriate to choose group spiritual direction. They may choose it in place of individual direction. I had been meeting with a directee for spiritual direction for several years. We decided that it might be good for him to try group spiritual direction. He had been the focus of attention in several different settings. Sometimes he seemed very preoccupied with himself and what he needed to receive. Often he just reported his experience and then looked to me for insight concerning it. I thought that in group spiritual direction he might come to a place of listening to the direction

God offered within his experience as he listened with others for this direction in their lives. I also thought that he might begin to claim the gift of giving as he committed himself to the prayerful support of others in the group process.

We agreed that we would continue to meet periodically just to see how things were going. The group proved to be the right place for his spiritual direction. After a while he no longer sought our individual meetings and I considered them unnecessary. The group offered the atmosphere and mutual companionship in which discernment could happen easily for him. He later wrote:

Through individual direction, my spiritual director helped me move from over-analysis and self-preoccupation to the simple question, "Have you brought it to prayer?" Or "What comes up for you when you pray about it?" Prayer became important to me. It became a more natural part of my life.

After two years my spiritual director suggested that I consider group spiritual direction. I reluctantly agreed to think about it and perhaps "pray" about it. My fear was of giving up individual attention. I was concerned that my unique spiritual needs would not be met.

Because I had always longed for a group to pray with and I trusted my spiritual director, I agreed to try the group. After a few months of getting acclimated, I began to look forward to it and have found it tremendously helpful. Hearing the spiritual journeys of others lends perspective to my journey. With the support of my group and their prayers, I am more open to stepping out in faith. I have made some difficult decisions that I don't think I could have made without that support.

Choosing Participants

A process for screening applicants can be helpful. In parish settings where people are accustomed to participating in any group they choose, screening may be difficult. But it is not impossible, especially if there are other options. If a pre-existing group such as a parish staff or a support group is considering group spiritual direction, it is important that every member of the group be committed to the process.

Publicity for the group should distinguish it from other kinds of groups. Include descriptions of other resources available to people such as reflection groups, Bible study groups, Cursillo accountability groups, prayer/faith sharing groups, and support groups. Such a listing will help people decide and avoid a sense of exclusivity about group direction. It can also be reassuring to persons who are hungering for some kind of supportive community by letting them know that there are possibilities for this besides group direction.

A phone or face-to-face interview can be helpful as part of the application process. Where this is not practical, the application might include two questions: "What attracts you to group spiritual direction at this time? Can you commit yourself to all the meeting dates?" If, after reading this response, you are concerned that some may not understand the purpose of the group or that the group may not be appropriate for them, you might call people to discuss your concerns. In talking with people about the group, I try to listen for the following:

Are individuals able to talk about their relationship with God? How God is relating to them? How they are relating to God?

It is helpful to have some sense of how comfortable individuals are with self-disclosure and whether they are in touch with the activity of God in their lives. Exploring this with people also gives some idea of their language, or lack of it, for articulating a faith response. Such information can be helpful when arranging groups.

How does group spiritual direction seem to fit with what is going on between applicants and God? What makes them think that group direction might be right for them?

Sometimes it never occurs to people to think about choices for spiritual enrichment from the vantage point of prayer. By posing the possibility that God may have a part in their consideration of the group you may offer fresh perspective on their choice.

What supports do people have for their lives now? Where can they talk about what is important to them?

Sometimes people have not felt the companionship of kindred spirits. If they hope the group can offer companionship in their life with God, group spiritual direction might be right for them. Discussion around this question can help ensure that an applicant is not looking to the group as a substitute for other ongoing support for life in general or as a life-line for his or her spiritual journey. Also, it can help assure prospective applicants that there will be no social obligations associated with group spiritual direction.

Are there any disturbing circumstances in the person's life now that consume most of their energy? Is the person looking for answers or solutions? Is the person able to pray about life circumstances? Does it seem that problem areas would get in the way of listening to others in the group or interfere with the process of the group?

Some considerations to keep in mind are: Is there a need for therapy rather than direction, or as an adjunct to it?[2] Is the person focusing on problems to escape a deepening relationship with God? Can he or she relinquish this focus? Could it be that the person is very ripe for spiritual direction, able to or at least wanting to be with God in the upheaval, but that the emotional or spiritual turbulence may kidnap the group? If this is true, one-to-one direction may be more appropriate at least for a time.

Has the person had any experience of spiritual direction? If so, how has he or she benefited? What are such persons looking for in the group that they have not found in individual direction?

Exploring the meaning of spiritual direction early on can help to lessen the possibility of confusion and frustration later. People may have been in spiritual direction before, but their definitions and experience of spiritual direction may be very different from what the group will offer. Their understanding of spiritual direction may, in fact, be incompatible with what you expect to be happening in the group.

If people plan to continue in individual direction while being in the group, it is important that they not make premature decisions about what they will share in the group and what they will bring to individual direction. If there are a limited number of places in groups, I give preference to people who are not currently in one-to-one direction.

Do people have experience with other spiritually focused groups such as Renew, Cursillo, 12-Step, Education for Ministry, Covenant Discipleship Groups, Prayer/Faith sharing groups? In group spiritual direction, what do they hope will be the same? different?

Discussing other groups people have been in offers another opportunity to clarify the purpose of the group. Also, by hearing the kinds of difficulties people raise concerning other groups, you might get an inkling of whether they will meet the same difficulties with this group. Some people are too easily distracted in a group setting. Others say they prefer just to listen in groups and don't want to share. Others comment that it is difficult for them not to be competitive in a group setting. Still others indicate that they find it hard to sort out what they need to take for themselves from the words of others.

Are people open to talking about themselves, their relationship with God, in a group setting? To inviting others to look at their life with them and offer their perspectives?

In group spiritual direction there has to be a capacity and willingness to share one's spiritual journey in a group setting for the purpose of discerning God's presence with the assistance of others in the group. This goes a step beyond faith-sharing, because it requires the vulnerability to share the faith dimension of people's lives and invite others to reflect on it with them. People who are accustomed to having others look to them for such assistance may not have the vulnerability to include others in their discernment. It may be hard to admit that they do not have all the answers. They may find it difficult to receive from others. Others may find self-disclosure in a group too difficult. For such persons, one-to-one direction may be preferable.

Are individuals comfortable or at least willing to move beyond the discussion of ideas about God and spiritual matters to the sharing of what actually goes on between themselves and God? How God seems to address them through their ideas and those of others, through their action? How they address God through their ideas or their actions?

Some people may prefer a group where they can discuss issues or theological concerns with like-minded people. Others may prefer the intellectual challenge of being with people who think differently. They would probably put more emphasis on content than on the implications of the content for their relationship with God as one would find in spiritual direction.

Can individuals commit themselves to all the meeting dates?

Group spiritual direction requires regular attendance by all participants. Some absenteeism is unavoidable. But frequent absences may indicate a lack of commitment to the process and be disruptive to the group. People with schedules that preclude the possibility of their participation in most meetings would do better to consider one-to-one spiritual direction where meetings can be scheduled with greater flexibility.

Do individuals know other persons who are applying for group direction now? Is there anyone they would want particularly to be or not be in their group?

If someone asks to be with people whom they know well, I try to check it out with the people involved. Many people prefer not to be in a group with close friends, spouses or co-workers. If people ask to be together, I talk with them about how this would support them in the purpose of the group.

Once when I was in a short-term group with people who knew me, I had the sense that it was hard for them to hear where I was with God around a particular issue related to work. I talked about my impatience and how hard it was for me to be prayerful about it. People tried hard to reassure me that my response to the situation was quite natural and that I shouldn't be so hard on myself. I didn't need them there as supportive friends. What I wanted instead was some help in exploring the underlying invitations in the situation and my resistance. At the end of our time together one person was able to say, "Because I know Rose Mary so well it was difficult for me to listen through to God in what she was saying. I kept wanting to put my own interpretation on it. I had to refrain from offering my interpretation and rely on God to speak to her." In this case the familiarity proved of benefit to the listening process. It invited a prayerfulness. At other times, when familiarity locks us into dependence on our knowledge of the person rather than on prayer, it gets in the way.

ARRANGING GROUPS

A two-and-a-half hour meeting allows a spaciousness for the unfolding of the process of group spiritual direction. A longer period taxes the listening capacity of most people. Four-week or five-week intervals between meetings honors the sacred space within each person where ultimately all discernment happens. It also allows for a continuity in the group's life together.

I suggest having four or at most five persons in a group to ensure time for the sharing of each person and also allow for the possibility of occasional absences. Three is a minimum to benefit from the collective wisdom available through the group process. If groups can meet bi-weekly, six members would be optimum to allow for three people sharing one week and three the next.

If all members of a large pre-existing group such as a parish staff or vestry/council decide they would like to be in group spiritual direction together, divide them into permanent sub-groups that meet simultaneously and begin and end with prayer together. If only part of the group wants to engage in group direction, discuss the effects of this decision on the cohesiveness of the entire group. Perhaps it would be better for individuals to look for groups outside that setting.

The actual choice of persons who will be together may happen in a variety of ways. If little information is available, participants might be assigned randomly. If there is sufficient time for participants to become acquainted with one another at a faith level before actually beginning the group direction, they might choose their own groups.

If you are arranging groups, consider whether there are people from the same geographic area who might want to continue to meet after formal group sessions have ended. In assigning groups, consider people who have asked to be together, or asked not to be together. In general, because of the vulnerability and freedom needed for the process, I would not assign spouses, friends, or colleagues to the same group unless they specifically asked to be together.

Once when I was interviewing spouses for group spiritual direction, the husband said he wanted to be in a group with his wife because they never had time to talk about significant matters together. In a separate conversation, his wife said she would not want to be in a group with her husband because she thought it might interfere with her freedom to talk about how she saw God in her family life.

DIVERSITIES AND SIMILARITIES IN GROUPS

Participation in group direction requires a growing trust in God's presence in the group in and through diverse personalities. People new to the process, however, may find it difficult to trust the experience of discernment in the group if there is seemingly no common ground of experience or language. Therefore it can be helpful to have at least one other person in the group with whom one senses some compatibility. In arranging groups, try to recall any aspects of your conversations with applicants that might assist such pairing. This is not to imply that one should strive for homogeneity in groups. In fact, when people are dealing with their relationship with God, homogeneity is rarely possible or desirable.

Diversity of articulation within the group can open people to fresh possibilities for encountering and responding to God. Also, such diversity can engender a reverence for the mystery of God who will not be contained by the confines of our experience. Sometimes even extreme personality differences among members can be the inspiration for reverence. People can be surprised by the way God is present for them even through people they don't like.

FACILITATORS

The first decision to make regarding facilitators is whether to have them. Some factors to consider are: Do people have a common understanding of spiritual direction and an appreciation for the process of group spiritual direction? How fixed has a group become in its way of being together in other settings? How well do individuals know one another and will this familiarity inhibit or encourage the trust needed to enter fully into the process?

At least in the beginning, I would encourage the presence of a facilitator who, in modeling group spiritual direction and taking over the mechanics of the group, can free participants to more easily enter into the spirit of the process. An alternative to a single facilitator might be the rotation of the task among participants from meeting to meeting, or even within a given meeting, so that every person will have a time for sharing. Or all the groups can meet in the same room for the first several meetings with a common facilitator to guide them through the process. Whatever choice is made, it should be clear that ultimately each group must assume responsibility for its way of being together. The faithfulness of the group to its purpose is not the responsibility of any single person but rather of all the members together.

If the group has a facilitator, it should be someone who honors the process and can engage others in it quickly. The best person for this role would probably not be someone who is used to dominant leadership. Nor will it necessarily be an experienced spiritual director. Spiritual directors might be better able to model the kinds of questions appropriate for spiritual direction and suggest words and images that may be helpful to those who haven't talked much about their spiritual life before. However, precisely because they are spiritual directors, they may assume and be given too much responsibility for the group. They may find it difficult to trust the discernment of those less experienced and therefore be reluctant to engage the group in a process of discernment for each person. They may forget that in group spiritual direction one's understanding of discernment is enhanced not only through articulating one's story and hearing a word from another, but also through hearing the stories of others and listening to what arises in their prayer as they hear others.

In our experience, the best facilitators are those who have a familiarity with or at least an appreciation for the dynamic of group spiritual direction and who are wise enough to know that this dynamic does not depend on their expertise. They are tentative in their approach to the group. They are willing to trust God more than they trust their sense of readiness as a facilitator. They also can trust the worry about lack of readiness to God. They are still close enough to the beginnings of their conscious spiritual journey to remember the struggle in claiming that journey and in trying to articulate it to others. Thus, they can be supportive of others who want to do the same. They know and acknowledge that they do not have a monopoly on the Holy Spirit and are ready to involve the group in the process of discernment early on.[3]

Facilitators' Meetings

An advantage to offering group spiritual direction in a setting where there are several groups is the rich opportunity to meet with other facilitators. At Shalem we have found it helpful for the facilitators to meet in prayer for a half hour before the large group gathers. Some of us may come with a concern that we anticipate might block our openness to God's presence in the group. We ask for prayer for that. Or we may just need to relax together in silence, being supportive of one another in our desire to be present to God. We also meet after the session to review how our time in the small group has been. If we have sensed ourselves as escaping God or being kidnapped by a problem in the group, we might talk about that. One facilitator said, "I really wasn't feeling well tonight and didn't have much energy to bring to the group. Sitting here in the silence, I realize that this evening is the first time that I've gotten out of the way so God can take over." Another said, "I find myself becoming very competitive with one person who seems to want to take over the group. I really can't be very prayerful when she is present. The group does a much better job with that person than I can." The other facilitators may ask about how the facilitator is with God in this competitive edge. They may ask about God's presence in the group, even when the facilitator is not very prayerful. Someone may ask if the facilitator has any indication that the person may not belong in the group or if it just seems to be a personality conflict.

After we have shared about our experiences in the group, we may discuss common group maintenance issues that we feel should be addressed in the large group gathering time. For example, if a content question dealing with such topics as decision making, spiritual disciplines, or praying with Scripture has been raised in several groups, we might talk about offering a teaching session around the topic before a regular session. Mostly, though, in those meetings after our groups, we come to know a little more tangibly "how much we seek with great desire to see God," and we celebrate our joy as that seeing is mediated in very diverse ways through our presence in groups.

No amount of preparatory prayer or careful strategizing can guarantee that our groups will be "successful." Ordinary ways of evaluating success don't apply. We are really talking about God's work and we do not know enough about God's work to evaluate it. In the end we are left to hope for an openness to God. We are left to trust that wherever two or three are gathered in a desire for openness something good will happen, not only for ourselves but for our world.

Chapter 6

Issues in Group
Spiritual Direction

"My concern was...to know whether they were a people gathered under the sense of the presence of God in their meetings...and the Lord answered my desire. I was affected and tendered with them.... The Meeting being ended, the peace of God...remained as a holy canopy over my mind."

Thomas Story[1]

To say that whenever a group gathers in a desire for openness something good will happen does not imply an absence of difficulties. Difficulties in group direction are bound to arise and some may need to be addressed directly. However, they should not become an overriding concern. Rather, they can test our seeking God together and be an invitation to trust God's seeking of us and God's presence with us.

The intention of seeking God together for one another gathers the group under that sense of the presence of God of which Thomas Story speaks. It becomes the litmus test for difficulties that come up in individuals and the group: How do the difficulties affect the seeking? Do they obscure it by preoccupation with group maintenance? In spite of, or perhaps because of the discomfort they induce, do the difficulties make the seeking more authentic, the trust in God more real?

Facilitators do not need to be well acquainted with psychological group theory and practice. In fact, too much regard for this could eclipse one's reverence for the grace operative in the group. Social dynamics such as personality conflicts, polarization, lack of common interests, poor self-esteem among group members, which could be destructive in other kinds of groups, may even be of benefit in group spiritual direction. It may be well, however, to have a psychological consultant who understands group spiritual direction with whom to discuss concerns about the group or individuals that seem to obstruct the group process.[2]

Difficulties with the Group as a Whole

A group may begin the process in earnest but later back away from the risk that is involved in continuing together. Although this is never discussed, the group stands firm in resistance. People begin to come late. They stay on the surface of issues, and the group permits it. People seem to take turns problem-solving, analyzing or intellectualizing, and no one in the group calls it for what it is. Although they are willing to begin their time with silence, they lose sight of the need for prayerfulness or are openly resistant to it through the remainder of the time. When the facilitator or others raise this issue or call for silence, they are met with genuine surprise: "Everything seems fine to me"; "I thought we were really getting to some interesting stuff"; "I like our conversations. They flow naturally. The silence interrupts my thinking." Eventually hard questions must be asked: How does what is going on support, reflect our attentiveness to God for one another? Have we shifted from being present to God for one another to being present to one another with only an occasional reference to God? What is the purpose of our conversations now? Are we colluding to avoid what we said we wanted to do together?

If the group has gradually taken on a new identity, this needs to be acknowledged. It might happen that people have not been aware that the group has shifted its focus. While they may appreciate what is happening now, or maybe are just more comfortable with it, they may also recognize that the need for spiritual direction which brought them to the group is not being met. Once the group is willing to face these possibilities, it can decide its future.

From a place of prayer individuals might re-examine what they want from this group and claim that for themselves. Once everyone has been heard, the group can decide if and why it wishes to continue and how it will function. Individuals are free to choose whether or not to remain in the group. If the group chooses something other than group spiritual direction, the facilitator would probably withdraw from the group.

Resistance is subtle and often hard to name. Signs that might point to resistance in one group may merely indicate in another group a lack of familiarity with the process. This is particularly true when a group seems to be reneging on its responsibility to care for the intentionality of the group, allowing such responsibility to fall solely on the facilitator or another in the group. In such situations it may be that the members, although obviously wanting to be in group spiritual direction, feel inadequate to the task of group spiritual direction. They defer to the facilitator. Here facilitators might gently yet firmly continue to draw people into the process, gradually withdrawing their own prominent leadership. Sometimes a group will continue to depend on a facilitator. This is especially true if members frequently interact with one another in other settings.

By the end of the first year of working with a group of seminarians, I felt they were well able to continue without me as a facilitator. They were reluctant to do so without me, though, saying, "We spend too much time together in other roles around the seminary to be able to keep the focus of the group without you. We tried it the two times you couldn't be with us. One time we ended up continuing a theological discussion that we had just left in class. The other time we evaluated our field placement process. We just can't pull it off by ourselves."

I often find that when individuals or groups have been particularly open and vulnerable with God in a given session, they tend to do some back-peddling in the next meeting. They may criticize the process, undermine the facilitator, or become very passive. Such behavior may be a sign that things are going almost too well. It reflects a natural part of the process of growing openness to God. When a group recognizes this it can be the source of real celebration. If such behavior persists, however, it may need special attention. People may feel that they have gone as far as they want to with the group for now. The only way they know to deal with this is to resist the process. The facilitator may need to help them say to God and to one another that they want a break.

Difficulties with Individuals

Just as group behaviors can sabotage the group's endeavor, individual behaviors can do the same. As with groups, it may not always be clear whether the behavior speaks of resistance or an inability to enter into the process. Individual resistance may show itself in various ways. People may resist the spiritual intimacy of the group. They may share only generalized issues or interesting stories. They may ask for advice or information from the group and respond to others in the same way. Others may ignore the commitment to prayerful listening by usurping the time allotted to others or forging ahead with conversation when the group is obviously moving into silence. Still others may try to refocus the intent of the group to meet different personal needs. They may initiate socializing outside the group sessions or may introduce causes for the group to espouse.

Obviously, such behavior needs to be addressed. The questions of when and how and by whom need to be prayed about by everyone in the group. Sometimes, especially if a person is resisting the facilitator rather than the group spiritual direction itself, others can do what the facilitator cannot. They can persistently ask very direct questions such as, "I liked the story you shared but what does it have to do with you and God?" "Are you aware that you always interrupt our silence? Can you tell me why you do that?" "Do you really want advice? I don't feel like I have advice to offer you and I know that is not what I want from you."

Continual need for group confrontation saps the energy of the group, making it difficult for spiritual direction to happen. At the end of each session, people might reflect on questions such as: "How is the confrontation affecting our prayerfulness? Are we, perhaps, becoming more concerned about controlling the behavior of this person than we are about listening to God?" and share whatever they can of this reflection with the group. Eventually, if there is no change in the person's behavior and it is apparent that he or she is becoming disruptive to the group's process, the facilitator must ask the person to leave the group. This is a difficult but necessary part of the facilitator's responsibility.

Some people, because of their emotional turmoil, do not belong in group spiritual direction. However, this may not be detected before the group begins. They want to be prayerful. They want to be aware of God. They sincerely want spiritual direction. But the clamor of their lives may prevent them from listening to God for themselves and others in a group. They refocus the group on themselves even in their responses to others. They bring issues to the group that are so loaded that they seduce the group into problem-solving or psychologizing. The group then finds it hard to be centered in God. There are three questions to consider in deciding whether or not such individuals should continue in a group:

How is their presence affecting them?

Perhaps the caring love of the group is freeing a person to turn a little more directly to the caring love of God outside the group. It also could be that the caring of the group is sheltering the person just enough that the needed psychological help is never sought.

How is their presence affecting others in the group?

It is important to note whether or not the person's behavior infringes on the time of spiritual direction for others in the group or disrupts the process of the group.

How is their presence affecting the intentionality of the group?

The presence of such individuals need not get in the way of the intentionality of the group. It may, in fact, be the catalyst for more authentic prayer in the group. It may call others in the group beyond their ordinary ways of caring. They may find that they have no choice but to entrust these individuals to God.

There is also the possibility that seemingly "just right" candidates get into group spiritual direction because they think they should. They have heard about the benefits of the group from participants whom they respect. They think it might be right for them but it just doesn't seem to fit. They are conscientious about their commitments and think they should "hang in" with the group. Well-meaning facilitators or groups may try to reshape the group to meet the needs of these people without any prayerful sense that this is appropriate or that the individuals want the group to change because of them. Perhaps the real gift of group direction in this situation is the opportunity to claim and reverence the different ways in which God seems to nurture the human heart.

One woman came to a group because she needed the prayerful support of the group. Once she was there, she realized that she was reluctant to talk about herself and that she really didn't want any feedback from the group. She said, "I didn't realize that our time together would include as much sharing as it does. I feel that I am in a very private place with God right now. It is hard for me to talk about this. I feel like I need your prayer more than I need your words to me. I also feel that I can better pray for you than offer my words." The group was willing to honor her request. They did ask that she share with them something of what seemed to come up in her prayer for herself. After several months she wanted to enter into the sharing more fully.

Reverence for diversity is a challenge for most groups. In the beginning one person may feel out of place because his or her way of being prayerful or his or her style of interaction is different from that of others in the group. One man, after observing the "real play" which included five women, said, "This closing your eyes stuff and whispered speaking? Does it mean that only women can do group direction?" Yet after several meetings with his own group, he came to realize that what is important is that people are seeking God for one another and not necessarily how they give expression to that seeking or what they look like when they are trying to be prayerful.

Another person had more difficulty in believing in the underlying unity present in great diversity. After hearing from people for several months, she felt there was no one in the group who could relate to her spiritual journey nor she to theirs. She tentatively shared her journey, then seemed to withdraw from the conversation of the group, occasionally interjecting a comment or question that came to her in the silence. She was willing, however, to be there prayerfully for the group. Through her sharing, she drew others beyond their parochial ideas about God to more expansive vistas. But she didn't know this. Others commented on the power of her prayerful presence for them and the appropriateness of her comments to them, but that was hard for her to imagine. As far as she was concerned she was a misfit. She was hesitant to say this in the group, afraid she would sound judgmental. Finally she said to me, "I just don't feel that there is a place for my God in this group."[3]

This person would probably do better in individual spiritual direction. In one-to-one direction, differences may exist, but as long as directors are free to receive directees where they are, the differences may not get in the way. Since in one-to-one direction directors usually only share about their own journey when it seems it may benefit directees, the directees may more readily feel that their uniqueness can be heard and appreciated.

Conclusion

Difficulties encountered in group spiritual direction should be dealt with in the context of intercessory prayer. When we want to be present to God for others, to enter into God's prayer for them, our responses may be very different from those of ordinary logic or psychological theory. The stance of intercessory prayer ultimately opens us to the peace of God. If, in fact, we find that "when the meeting being ended this peace of God...remained as a holy canopy over our minds," then something very good has happened whether or not we can name it. That peace extends from us to our world.[4]

Chapter 7

The Contemplative Dimension of Group Spiritual Direction

"Contemplative prayer brings us directly into contact with what is, and thus directly into one another's hearts and the heart of the world."

Wendy M. Wright[1]

Group spiritual direction can be a form of contemplative prayer. It is a communal and individual offering to God of time together, asking to assist one another in seeing "what is." There is a vulnerability involved in group spiritual direction. We are asked to share our spiritual hearts with others and be open to receiving what others offer of themselves. As we come in touch with the Mystery of God in the depths of our being and that of others in the group, we come in contact with the "heart of the world" with whom we share this Mystery.

The following practices can prepare people for the seeing and the listening required for group spiritual direction. Some will introduce the faith sharing which flows out of people's sensitivity to God's presence in their lives and in the world. People may experiment with these practices alone. Often, though, the support of a group encourages people to trust themselves to God in the practice. A group leader might include some of these practices within the context of already existing groups. Since many people commit themselves to coming to denominational gatherings such as Sunday worship in order to be nurtured in their spiritual lives, such gatherings could well be the most natural setting in which contemplative practices such as these are introduced.

Silence

Many contemplative practices are grounded in silence. As stated in Chapter 4, many people have difficulties with silence. To them it may seem both unnatural and unproductive. When people are new to silence, there are not many words that can make sense of it for them, nor can they rely on others' experience. They need to try it for themselves. If people can see the choice to enter into silence as what we might do to consciously make space for God, the choice itself can be a prayer.

Parishes can introduce people to silence.[2] At parish liturgies, leaders might intersperse pauses throughout the service. It is important that people know that the silence is intentional and not just time for leaders to catch their breath or remember what they should be saying. The leader should prepare people for these pauses ahead of time, suggesting that people use them for the listening prayer of reflecting on the Scriptures or other words they have heard, offer silent prayer, or simply be present to God in their own ways.

Parish meetings might include some silence before the beginning spoken prayer. This silence can be a way of honoring the fact that the group would like to give God charge of the meeting; it can also provide time for people to claim their personal prayer for this intention. There might be silent pauses throughout the meeting, perhaps signaled by a bell, for people to return to their desire to be open to God's guidance. People might be encouraged to ask for some silence during the meeting if they feel they are losing sight of God in their deliberations.

This practice of silence might be continued at home and at work. The silence might be a way of expressing a desire for God and returning to that desire frequently. Individuals might start the morning with a few moments of "unproductive" silence, before the plans for the day's activities begin. They might also choose some reminders for silence throughout the day—familiar sounds like the chiming of a clock, the ringing of the phone or doorbell, the call of a child, or familiar images like a picture, a candle, a plant, or even a smudge of dirt. Even a bodily sensation like anger or pain can serve as a reminder. Such silences are not meant to insure that everything will go smoothly or that desired outcomes will be accomplished. The practice has no end other than a spaciousness for God. Gradually it expands our capacity for awareness of God in all of life.

Gentle Awareness

The awareness of God in all of life involves being present to life just as it is. Simple practices enable this presence. People might begin by taking five minutes periodically throughout the day just to stop and listen to the sounds around them—sounds of nature, of family, of office machines, of traffic. They might offer this time to God, asking God to open their ears to all of life.

In group settings people can be helped into this listening by hearing various sounds together, like the sound of a bell ringing, noticing the various tones of the ring as it fades into the silence. A leader might call the group's attention to the chirping of birds outside or laughter in an adjoining room. There is nothing to do with this listening except to listen. Eventually people may become aware of sounds that surround them all the time, sounds they haven't really heard before. They might notice the silence that is behind or underneath all the sound. They may be comfortable resting in that silence for a moment, letting things be as they are. Some may say that the silence isn't really silence because there is so much inner noise. Perhaps if they can listen with gentle ears to the noise, without trying to push it out, they may soften its harshness. They may come to view the noise as a passing cloud in the sky of silence.

Another practice that can assist awareness and presence is looking at oneself and one's surroundings with gentle eyes. A group leader might invite people to observe a candle, a plant, or any object in the room they want to look at, seeing it at first in its entirety, then carefully observing every detail of it. The leader might challenge the group to see the object as it is without thinking of how they would like it to be. After a few minutes of observation, people might journal about what they see, trying to do this without choosing their words or judging what they see. If there is time for sharing, people might share a brief descriptive word or phrase. Alone, individuals might begin by asking God to help them appreciate all of life, then look out a window for a few minutes, noticing what there is to be seen in the panorama of their vision. They might shift their focus to include friends and the people with whom they live or work. In this their prayer might be to see these people as they are and appreciate them, without needing to change them.

We might also extend the practice of contemplative awareness to include ourselves. Our beginning prayer could be Psalm 139: "For the wonder of myself I give you thanks," or another authentic prayer: "God, let me appreciate myself as you do." "Take away the fear I have of being with myself." After that, we might spend a few minutes looking in a mirror, seeing first the broad strokes of the face and then its detail. We might notice what it feels like, looks like to smile or frown. At another time we might spend a few minutes watching our breath, perhaps noticing our chest or abdomen rise and fall as the breath goes in and out, or feeling the coolness of the air as it passes through our nostrils. Or we might watch a particular feeling in us like anger, sadness, joy, or a bodily sensation like pain. Our prayer might be one of simple gratitude for the gift of life, or the honest expression of dissatisfaction with our appearances or the way our body functions. Thoughts about what one sees are not necessary. In fact, thoughts might get in the way of seeing what is really there. The goal of the practice is not to judge or to change anything. The goal is simply to observe and be aware and open our awareness to God. In opening our awareness to God we might pray for gentle eyes with which to see ourselves and all of creation. Such practices might sharpen our vision to see what is there in all of reality.

Faith-Filled Listening

The listening required in group spiritual direction implies a willingness to listen to God's Spirit in ourselves, in others, in the holy sources of our faith, in the events of our lives and our world, in all creation. Filled with expectancy, this listening is an act of faith in God's promise to us, "When you seek me you will find me. When you seek me with all your heart, I will let you find me."[3] Yet the listening is not limited by narrow expectations of how God's Spirit will manifest itself.

Many people seem inclined to look to others and to the holy sources of their faith first for God's revelation. They might ask another to look with them at the events of their lives to see what God is trying to tell them but seldom, without strong encouragement and assistance, do they look within themselves for inspiration and guidance. Ideally life itself offers the impetus for this. There may come the point when there is no one around to give answers or when another's answers are clearly not on target for the person seeking. Then that person is forced to turn to her or his inner resources. Hopefully this can be a positive choice to listen to God's Spirit within, acting as though one believes the words of Jesus telling us that the Holy Spirit who will teach us all truth is in us and will be with us forever.[4]

There are some practical things that can be done in parishes and group settings to help people honor the belief in the Spirit's presence within us. In worship services, liturgies, or wherever the Word of God is broken open, the worship leader or homilist might invite people into a few minutes of silence to hear God's word to them through the Scripture before the sermon is preached. Or the sermon might end with a question or a guided meditation that leads people into some quiet time with God. Bible study groups might offer similar opportunities. Sessions might include, along with input and sharing related to the understanding of a text, some silent time for reflection when people can invite God to address them through their ideas and the group discussion.[5] Spiritual formation groups, where forms of prayer or spiritual disciplines are taught, might consistently include space and questions for personal discernment such as, How does this practice fit with my experience of God? Does this practice honor and reflect my experience of God? Which of these disciplines will most support my spiritual journey now?

If opportunities for personal listening are not provided within group settings, participants should create the space for themselves. They might pray over the Sunday lessons before going to church, listening to God address them through the Word. Or, rather than listen to every word of a talk or sermon, they might choose to move into their hearts when a story or idea or question hits home. Or they could ask themselves at the end of a homily, How do these words fit my experience of God? or ask God, What are you wanting to say to me through this person? Within a very busy Bible study class or spiritual formation group, people might create an inner silence where they can be listening to God's word for them amidst the busyness.

Although a group can support its members in the practice of faith-filled listening, this practice cannot be limited to times in groups. Eventually it must become a way of life, a habit wherein we view and hear all of life through the eyes and ears of faith. We grow in sensitivity to God's presence with us in all of life. Intentional quiet time for open presence to God and prayerful reflection on one's day foster this sensitivity to God. Together these two practices could be the envelope that enfolds each day in our desire for God.

Open Presence

Open presence to God means just that. It is the time one takes to be present to God without agenda or without pre-conceived notions of what should happen. One might begin this open presence prayer by expressing one's desire to be present for whatever God would have, or by expressing one's fear or apprehension about being with God without specific things to say or do, whatever prayer is authentic. One might be aware of pain or agitation or joy and open this to God without trying to fix it, push it away, or do anything with it.

This prayer may not always feel good. We may feel that we are wasting time, that we should be doing more in prayer. And this may be true, but it is more likely that such thoughts are a subtle temptation to take control of the time. At other times of the day something very different may be called for: prayers of tears, of petition, of work, of deciding. But for now a spaciousness in which we are aware of God's presence in us is all that is needed.

Daily Reflection on Life

The second practice, daily reflection on life, acknowledges the reality that as much as we might want to be aware of God in all of life, we often miss God's presence with us. This practice is grounded in the faith assumption that God really is present with us in every moment of our lives, even the seemingly insignificant ones. We look back with God at the events and relationships of each day, not thinking about the day but bringing it to our prayer. We ask for God's perspective on what has been going on. It's like sitting down with God and watching a video of our day, with God as the commentator. We might begin to notice what we had missed through the day: the way God was present for us through the most difficult circumstances or some of the very ordinary moments; occasions when we chose to take things into our own hands, shutting out God; the people and tasks that helped us remember God; moments of faith or joy that we didn't savor at the time.

As we come to the end of the video, we might talk with God about what we have seen. There may be people from the day whom we want to bring into our prayer. There may be unfinished business that we want to entrust to God or resolve to address in some other way the next day. We might simply be present in whatever authentic prayer is evoked by the experience. As we end our reflection on the day, we might run a preview of the next day. In doing so, we may remember some specific challenges which will face us. Rather than trying to figure out how we will deal with the challenges, we can open our concern to God, asking God to keep us turned toward God in the midst of the challenges. We might try to think of ways that will help us remember God during the day.

Journaling about the awarenesses that flow from this prayer can help clarify our experience of God. Some people journal in complete sentences, others use only phrases or key words, still others journal through poetry or art. We might ask God to guide this process and then record the awareness as it is, without judging or pushing for interpretation. Reflecting on our journal periodically, and especially in times of transition, can help us notice patterns of God's invitations and our response or resistance that we might otherwise miss.

Humble Faith Sharing

Faith sharing is an essential part of group spiritual direction. It is the practice in which two or more people share experiences concerning their relationship with God: their awareness of God's Presence in the events of their lives; their struggles to believe in God's Presence; the ways in which they have responded to or resisted God's Presence in their lives; places of suffering, confusion, or joy that have been the entry point for their prayer. It is grounded in humble acceptance of the truth that each of us is a person honored and loved by God and that God is present and active in all of our lives. It assumes the belief that God often chooses to minister to us through the sharing and support of others.

Intentional faith sharing is done in an atmosphere of reverent listening and confidentiality, surrounded by prayer. People are asked to share their experiences simply and to receive the sharing of others without judgment or attempts to change the experience. There are numerous possibilities for the content of what is shared. It may include a single incident in a person's life or a time of longer duration. It may also include response to things such as Scripture, a film, or some form of prayer experienced with a group. In group spiritual direction, after the faith sharing of each person, there is usually a time of dialogue in which the group helps the person further clarify her or his experiences. In faith sharing per se, the sharing of each person is followed only by a prayerful silence during which the group holds the person in prayer. If there is any dialogue, it comes only after everyone has shared. It is generally related to the common experience of the group rather than the experiences of specific individuals.

In the beginning, people may need help to share their experience of God. Group leaders might incorporate silence and a few questions for people to respond to in small groups at the beginning of a meeting. Simple, direct questions that invite concrete contained responses are usually easiest to deal with. In a parents' meeting, for instance, questions might be: What experience have I had with my children in the past few months that has made me pray more? or What are my children teaching me about God? or How much do I trust God to care for my children? The meeting might end with a few minutes of silence and then the question which people might respond to aloud: How would I like people to pray for me? What is my prayer for myself? for my children?

A parish vestry meeting might begin with questions like: How has God come alive for me through my participation in the life of this parish? or What are some events in my life over the past months that have invited me to pray more? A staff meeting might begin with questions such as: What helps me most to remember God here at work? or What is my over-all sense of how I have been present/wanted to be present to God through this month? When have I chosen autonomy rather than companionship with God? or How can people here support me in living out of my desire for God at work? A Bible study group might begin with a questions like: Can I remember a time this week when the Sunday lessons had particular meaning for me because of what was going on in my life? Eventually, faith sharing might become a more natural part of our relationships with at least a few people.

Sometimes a group will set aside time on a regular basis for extended faith sharing. In such instances, a group of six or seven would probably gather for a minimum of an hour and a half. The group might work out guidelines for itself, such as how frequently they will meet for faith-sharing, how they will share the leadership of the group, how they will remind one another of their reason for being together, and how they will divide their time together. A clergy support group, for example, might decide to use one meeting each quarter to share their experiences of God in ministry. They might have a half hour of silence which is introduced with a Scripture reading, then forty-five minutes for faith sharing and conclude with fifteen minutes of shared prayer. Other possibilities for such groups are:

A group of friends or members of the same parish might meet once a month for this kind of sharing. They decide ahead of time that the question/topic around which they share will be determined by the leader and that the question or topic should be introduced in a way that invites faith sharing rather than theological discussion. They gather in silence for thirty minutes during which time the leader reads a Scripture like John 1 where Jesus is asking two disciples, "What do you want?" The leader leaves the group with this question for themselves. As they come to the end of the silent time, the leader might ask people to share, if they can, how they answered that question for themselves. People might share a statement or a few sentences related to the question but with no verbal response from the group. At the end of the sharing, the leader might ask people how they would like the group to pray for them during the next month. The group could end with shared petitions for their families and the world.

Another group might model its sharing on Lectio Divina,[6] the centuries-old practice of the slow, reverent reading of the Scriptures which moves the heart to prayer. This format would include three different readings of the same Scripture passages, preferably from different translations. People gather in open silence for about twenty minutes, then listen to the first reading of the Scripture. After some silence, members share a word or phrase from the reading that touched them. After a few minutes more of silence, another translation of the same passage is read and people share a brief prayer response to what they have heard. The third reading of the passage, from yet another translation, is followed by extended silence. The group ends with twenty minutes of open shared prayer.

Faith sharing is a way of helping us claim and clarify our experience of God. The praying presence of others as we claim our experience can support us in living out our faithful response to God. Hearing another's experience of God can enhance our appreciation for the myriad ways in which God is actively engaged in the world and in all creation. We grow in reverence for ourselves and others and all that is in the universe. We recognize that we are one in God and that "in God, all are sacred."[7] This recognition becomes an invitation to hospitable prayer; it is also the fruit of such prayer.

Hospitable Prayer

Much of this book has been devoted to intercessory prayer. Hospitable prayer is another way of speaking of this. It is prayer that acknowledges our solidarity with all creation. It is prayer that joins us consciously with all creation as we enter into our prayer. It is prayer that is open to receiving those people or circumstances given us by God for our prayer.

Often hospitable prayer is the fruit of other contemplative practices, such as those described above. Sometimes this prayer can be cultivated through specific practices.[8] Some practices of hospitable prayer might be:

- taking time at the beginning of intentional prayer to be mindful of the communion of saints, all those holy people living and deceased who share a desire for God;
- praying John 17, Jesus' prayer for oneness, gradually expanding your awareness beyond self, friends, enemies, the world, to include your oneness with all of creation;
- dedicating a time of prayer or work for another person or some world circumstance;
- asking God whom/what God would have us pray for and how God would have us pray; allowing space for God's prayer for this person or circumstance to be prayed in us;
- pausing throughout the day to turn to the four directions of the earth to bless and be blessed by all creation;
- dedicating the fruits of one's spiritual practices for the well-being of others;

- praying the daily news by pausing to pray for those situations in the newspaper or televised news that claim our attention;
- dedicating the time of meetings for others;
- sharing petitions for the world which come out of silence at the end of meetings.

Conclusion

Although this chapter has been titled "The Contemplative Dimension of Group Spiritual Direction," the practices described in it need not be viewed only as preparation for group spiritual direction. In fact, whether or not a person chooses to enter group spiritual direction is secondary to one's contemplative awareness. This awareness is our direct contact with what is *and thus with one another's hearts and the heart of the world.*[9] In this place of hospitality we can pray God's prayer for us and for our world.

Epilogue

"We are far from realizing all that human spirits can do for one another on spiritual levels if they will pay the price."

Evelyn Underhill[1]

What is the price of which Evelyn Underhill speaks? It is, I think, the price of intercessory prayer. It is a price we pay for those whom we love. Often we do not know its effects.

As I come to the end of this writing, I am aware of the many people who are paying this price for me, who are standing in the presence of God for me. Occasionally these people will tell me they are praying for me. They also express interest in what I am doing. They seldom ask if I am finished with my book.

The gift of intercessory prayer is concretized for me in two friends particularly. One who knew that I was writing on a given day called me in the middle of the day. He simply said, "Hi, Rose Mary! I hope the writing is going O.K. I'm praying for you." I was able to continue my writing in the promise of his prayer.

The other friend has been staying with me for several weeks. Each morning, as I sit and write, I am aware that she is in another room praying. She seldom talks about her prayer but I have the feeling that it includes me. Her faithful presence holds me in the presence of God as I write.

One morning during my own prayer time I heard the words, "Let your writing be your prayer." That invitation has changed the way I write. My writing is no longer a means to a finished product. Instead, it has become an expression of my willingness to be present in the moment, waiting for whatever might be given. The writing has become an act of intercessory prayer also.

I offer it for those who will read my words and for those who will participate in group spiritual direction.

The attitude of intercessory prayer is nurtured in settings like group spiritual direction. Here people are present to God for others in the group. Here, as participants in group spiritual direction attest, they are gifted by the praying presence of others:

> "Although I went into group spiritual direction a little skeptical, it has been just what I needed. I have grown closer to God through the presence of some wonderful people. I continue to pray for them." (Episcopal priest)

> "I have been wounded by relationships in the past and have tended to withdraw into myself. There is a gentle strength in the group that has been healing. I have become more trusting of God in other relationships." (Episcopal priest)

> "Praying with others and for others is an act of love. It has taught me a great deal about love and intimacy. It is difficult for me to put into words the closeness I feel for friends that I only know through praying together. God's love is vividly present when we meet. I believe we all grow as lovers in the process. This love has helped me make some difficult decisions that I couldn't have made alone." (Roman Catholic legal consultant)

> "The group experience is a blessing—an oasis—in my busy life. It challenges me to listen prayerfully. As I am able to do this in other places like church council meetings, I am more likely to speak from my God-center." (Lutheran music therapist)

> "By being part of the group I have become more aware of God in my day-to-day existence. I am challenged back into prayer and awareness when I have gotten caught up in the busyness of work." (Episcopal pediatrics anesthesiologist)

> "I have learned that I can be actively in prayer for any person I am dealing with, in whatever circumstance." (Roman Catholic publisher)

> "At times when I felt empty and low, and felt I couldn't pray, it was helpful to know that people were praying for

me. Even when I had to be away, I felt a part of the group. I knew the people were praying for me. I could ask myself the question they would ask: "Where is God for you in your work?" (Unitarian Universalist conference coordinator)

"It was helpful for me to be with a group other than my religious community. I felt free to examine my vocation in a way that I could not do within my community. As I leave to go to a new assignment, I know my group will be praying for me." (Roman Catholic seminarian)

"Group spiritual direction provides a time for me to sit with God and look at my life, the good and the bad. I know that I can talk with God about all of my experiences." (American Baptist counselor)

"Three of us in our group are at major crossroads in our lives. We have been struck by the similarities among us—we are all wrestling with issues of personal identity, change, uncertainty, apprehension, and trust in God. That we have been able to pray together and share our experiences has been a great, great blessing of our spiritual encounter." (Greek Orthodox graduate student)

"Being in group spiritual direction has changed my approach to life in general. Even when I am sitting in faculty or vestry meetings I find I can pray for those who are with me and the work we are doing together." (Episcopal teacher)

"Group spiritual direction has affected the way I approach my family. I find, for example, that I am no longer trying to change my daughter. I can accept her as she is and pray for her." (Church of the Brethren seminary professor)

Although the attitude of intercessory prayer often has its conscious beginnings in group spiritual direction, it is not limited to that experience. As we are "gentled" into God's caring love by those who hold us in love, we come to trust it in many diverse situations. We are willing to risk the implications of love even through our fear or defensiveness. Gradually we come to be at home in the Heart of Love. Our hearts expand to embrace our brothers and sisters. We can love them with a detached compassion which is willing for whatever God invites us to in their behalf. We can pray that love be done for all the world, for all creation. The gift of intercessory prayer will be a hospitable heart.

Having experienced the gift of intercessory prayer in group spiritual direction, for myself and others, I begin to see its potential for transforming our nation, our world. I begin to wonder, to dream:

What would our nation become if Americans took seriously the responsibility to pray for our leadership? Would the grid-locking in Congress cease if its members were willing to be in prayer together? How would they listen and respond to the needs of the poor, the elderly, gays and lesbians if they held these people in intercessory prayer? How would they share the resources of our country with other less fortunate nations if they asked God's direction?

How would peace negotiators approach their efforts toward peace if they began to trust God more than they trusted their strategies? Would peace finally come to the Middle East, Bosnia, Serbia, South Africa and other strife-torn countries if their peoples were willing to pray for God's compassion? How would the rest of the world be changed if we held the people of these nations in prayer?

What would happen if leaders of world religions acknowledged their shared desire for God? Would their concern for differences disappear? If they entered into the prayer of Jesus for unity, "May they all be one," might they recognize that we have, forever, all been one in God?[2]

I can only begin to envision a world where the power of intercessory prayer is brought to bear on it. I suspect that boundaries which protect our interests and defend us from one another will not be needed. Instead there will be one spiritual community where all live together in the caring love of God. Then there will be no need for the structures of group spiritual direction. Wherever people are gathered they will gather in an openness to God for one another, for all creation. They will be willing to pay the price of intercessory prayer.

Appendix:
Group Spiritual Direction
as Support for Ministry

"Two are better than one...for if they fall, one will lift up the other."

Ecclesiastes 4:9-10

Guidelines

These guidelines are adapted from Peer Group Guidelines for Spiritual Directors used by Shalem Institute for Spiritual Formation. They are offered as a model of group spiritual direction especially for those in pastoral ministries such as spiritual renewal, health care, adult religious formation, and catechesis. People in other workplace settings who wish to deepen their presence for God in the workplace may find this model of group spiritual direction useful also.

I. Guidelines for Beginning a Group: Selection of Group Members

The group should be comprised of yourself and at least three other people who are in the same or a similar ministry. There probably should be no more than six or seven people in the group. It is well to form as heterogeneous and ecumenical a group as possible or at least include people from various ministry settings.

It is ideal to have a balanced range of faith traditions, sex, experience in the ministry, etc. The broader this range, the more able group members will be to address each other's blind spots and the wider will be the scope of perception and language. If differing terminologies prove to be confusing rather than helpful, the group may need to meet an extra time or two simply to share understandings and language. In order to insure some compatibility among group members, you might find it helpful to explore with potential members what is at the heart of ministry for them and what they would most want from a group like this.

The most important considerations in selecting a group member are:

A. Is the person actively involved in the ministry, full or part time, paid staff or volunteer?

B. Is the person wanting to be part of the group in order to deepen her/his awareness and responsiveness to God in this ministry as opposed to enhancing his/her skills or knowledge?

C. Is the person able to give and receive in a group without needing to take charge?

D. Is the person's schedule flexible enough to allow him/her to attend all the meetings once the group has set up dates?

Responsibility of the Person Organizing the Group

The ongoing functioning of the group is dependent upon the group but there are some responsibilities which the person organizing the group will need to assume:

A. Organize the group and make sure everyone understands the purpose, content and process.

B. Lead the initial meeting during which the guidelines are reviewed and meeting times, places, facilitators and presenters are scheduled. Leadership of subsequent meetings will be the job of the assigned facilitator.

C. Oversee changes in scheduling or membership.

Meeting Schedule

Meetings should be scheduled approximately monthly, for a minimum of ninety minutes each, except for the first meeting which should be two hours. If a group is also meeting for extended faith sharing, support for ministry, etc., it will be necessary to plan a separate time for this or to extend the meeting time so the time needed for presentations can be honored.

The Initial Meeting

This initial session should include time for personal faith-sharing among the members, sharing of expectations and concerns, and corporate prayer as well as the business of orientation and scheduling of subsequent meetings. Members should have copies of these guidelines in advance of the meeting in order to save time and to give members a chance to reflect on them before coming together. Make sure all the members bring their calendars to this meeting. If you wish, you might want to use something like the following agenda, which others have found helpful for the first meeting:

A. Opening—you open the meeting and make any necessary introductions.

B. Beginning prayer—perhaps a period of about fifteen minutes of quiet, with Scripture or some other reading, shared prayer, etc. (It is very important that the group start experiencing prayer together as soon as possible.)

C. Review of the agenda.

D. Your sharing of your spiritual pilgrimage and how it has led you to this ministry; your understanding of the nature of your ministry and the way you see the group serving your spiritual journey within the ministry; your hopes, fears and expectations for the group.

E. Sharing of group members, introducing themselves, describing something of their personal spiritual journeys, their sense of calling to the ministry, their hopes and fears and expectations for the group.

F. Some time for reflections by anyone on general themes which have surfaced, or any specific responses they wish to make.

G. Scheduling monthly meetings and establishing the meeting place(s).

H. Establishing a schedule for facilitators and presenters on a rotational basis or decide on a manner agreeable to all for doing so on an ongoing basis. (Some groups choose to do this at the end of each meeting rather than for an entire year.)

I. Any other business.

J. Ending with prayer.

II. Guidelines for the Group

Purpose

The purpose of these meetings is to provide all group members with consistent ongoing support for their spiritual journeys as it affects and is affected by their ministries. All will present situations or vignettes from their ministries, with the focus being on the presenter rather than on the people who might be involved in the situation, and the group will reflect prayerfully upon these presentations, expressing any feedback, affirmation, questions and insights that seem appropriate. The recommended schedule includes one presentation/discussion period in each ninety-minute monthly meeting. From time to time the group may choose to discuss an issue common to all their ministries rather than have a presentation.

Group Atmosphere

The most important thing to understand about the group is that it should be conducted with a prayerful, reverent, contemplative attitude. If group members are going to help one another be attentive to God in their ministries, they need to try to be attentive to God during the meetings themselves. For this reason, care should be given to holding the group in a way and place that encourages an open, calm atmosphere, and the group should learn to pray together comfortably. Time will be needed for the members to become trusting of one another and to relax together. This trust may be assisted by including in each meeting a brief time at the beginning for optional faith-sharing around one's experience of God in ministry. The members should actually be spiritual friends to one another during the meetings. It is helpful if everyone nurtures an attitude of intercessory prayer, i.e. being available to God for one another.

Specifically, this means that each member's attitude would be "contemplative," a relaxed but very attentive listening to one another and to one's own inner responses, and looking for the presence of the Holy Spirit in what is happening moment-by-moment. Normally, this involves a willingness to refrain from leaping into the discussion with the first thing that comes to mind; to stand back a bit and try to sense and respond to the Spirit's movement, allowing responses to surface gently rather than grasping for them. Anything that the group finds helpful to this attitude should be encouraged.

Ample time for prayer at the beginning is very important, and silent times of prayer during the discussion also help. Some groups find it important to hold their meetings in "holy space," have a candle lit, or use some other physical cues as reminders to be attentive to God's presence in the meetings.

During the meetings, this prayerful atmosphere and attentiveness to the Divine is likely to be disrupted by a number of things. It may be disrupted by self-consciousness, a need to appear competent or to get one's point across, fear of criticizing or of being criticized, need to solve problems, analyze situations, or to offer "help," to discuss an issue raised by the presenter theoretically rather than staying focused on the presenter's concerns in the issue. Such distractions are bound to occur from time to time, and it is unrealistic to expect to maintain a constant contemplative attitude in any setting. However, it is possible to keep reminding oneself of the priority of the Divine, and thus to call oneself "back" to this essential Center whenever attention has been taken away. It should be the responsibility of each group member to attend to his or her own awareness in this way and also to keep noticing the overall atmosphere of the group to see if some correction might be needed.

For example, if it appears that the discussion has drifted too far into problem-solving or analysis, the first member to notice this should bring it to the group's attention. Perhaps she or he could say, "I wonder if we're staying on target here—it seems to me that we're filling all the space with words," or "How do you sense the presence of the Lord in our discussion right now?" or "Could we pause for a few moments of silence at this point?" or "Maybe we need to set aside time to talk about this as an issue together. But for now could we stay focused on the presenter's concerns in this?" Taking even a few seconds of prayer or simple silence in the midst of a group discussion can be a very effective way of recentering everyone's attention. The silences and spaces in group meetings may well prove more helpful than all the words that are said.

It can be seen that the attitude encouraged in these group meetings is very different from that found in either psychological "case presentations" or theological "discussion groups." In such groups, emphasis is usually placed on psychological analysis, problem-solving, or intellectual understanding. Although a bit of this may legitimately occur from time to time in group spiritual direction, the real goal for each member should be to gently try to hear and respond to God's presence, the movement of the Spirit within the meeting itself.

Content of the Meetings

Each meeting should be carefully centered around experiences and concerns relating specifically to the involvement of the presenter in ministry, and focused on **how the prayer experience and faith life of the presenter is impinging upon and being affected by ministry or a situation in ministry**. Specifically, the group should try to keep the focus on the presenter's spiritual concerns, experiences, feelings, faith, blocks, blind spots, gifts, discernments, confidence and confusions in relation to the situation in ministry rather than on "what to do in this kind of situation" or "how to solve the presenter's problem." This focus will be assisted by the presenter including something about his or her prayer and discernment around the situation and asking the group for help with his or her own reflections about these specific spiritual concerns rather than seeking advice or suggestions. While there may be occasions where some kind of focus on the situation or some problem-solving is clearly called for, this should be kept to a minimum, and it should never be allowed to eclipse the focus on the spiritual awareness of the presenter. Nor should it distract the group from their immediate, moment-by-moment attentiveness to the Divine.

This will necessitate a carefully organized and planned presentation including **only** enough information about the situation to provide an adequate understanding of the presenter's experience of it. The best single guideline in preparing presentations is for the **presenter to plan to present** *herself or himself* **in relation to the situation, and not to present the situation as a "case."** It is also recommended that the presenter develop some *questions* for the group about the spiritual concerns related to the situation by stating specific issues about which feedback is desired. It should be understood that presentations do not need to contain "problems" to be solved. In a number of instances, the situation may be going very well, and the required feedback may be nothing more than affirmation of and gratitude for this fact. On the other hand, if there do seem to be some problems or blocks, they should be identified and confronted with as much candor as possible. The presenter can help the group keep the focus on the spiritual life of the presenter rather than on problem solving, advice giving, or discussion of issues by avoiding questions like: "What has been your experience in this?" or "What have you done in similar situations?" or "Do you have any ideas on what I should do?"

The anonymity of other people must be preserved whenever possible, and always when the situation involves a relationship of confidentiality. To this end, presenters should change any possibly identifying data (name, occupation, location, etc.) when presenting relationships of confidentiality.

Since the focus is on the presenter, it is not essential to know everything about the situation or persons involved. On the other hand, whatever of the situation the presenter is specifically concerned about should be presented accurately. **Always** use fictitious names in the presentation.

The presentation can include a specific situation in ministry or an overall sense of one's ministry as it has developed over time, a brief verbatim account of a moment that seemed especially graced or especially problematic, or a follow-up of a situation that has been previously presented. If you are choosing to present a situation, you may want to choose one which has some ongoing significance in your ministry or is apt to be encountered again. It is up to the presenter to decide what material to present, and what form this should take. Again, this calls for careful, prayerful reflection ahead of time.

It will help both the presentation and subsequent discussion if the presenter includes the following reflections in the presentation:

1. How do I feel about myself in this situation or this ministry?
2. How have I been praying
    a. For the persons involved in my ministry or in this situation?
    b. For the situation?
    c. For myself?
3. What seems to happen in this prayer?
4. What is my sense of prayer while I'm in this situation or involved in this ministry?
5. How do I sense/think/feel God at work in this situation or this ministry?

The subject of the presentation is the **presenter**—and most specifically the *spiritual life* of the presenter as it is reflected and affected in the situation/ministry presented.

The purpose of this format is twofold. The first is to focus on the assumption that fruitful ministry is more than having the proper credentials and skills and knowing the right techniques to handle a given situation. Instead, **it is a matter of clearing the blocks within the presenter so that he or she can be clearly and**

immediately present to the reality of the Holy Spirit, available for whatever might be called for in the moment.

The second purpose of this format is to honor and protect the intent of the group spiritual direction for the presenter. If it ever seems necessary for the group to focus on skills or general issues related to ministry, the group might choose ahead of time to devote one meeting to that.

Role of Facilitators

Facilitators and presenters should be scheduled on a rotational basis, with one facilitator and presenter for each meeting. It is best **not** to attempt to use the same person as facilitator and presenter. It is the responsibility of the facilitator to open and close each meeting, to lead prayer time, to keep time carefully according to the agenda, to moderate the discussion as needed, and to attend to whether the discussion is following the intent, atmosphere and attitude described in these guidelines. (This latter is of course everyone's responsibility, but it helps to have the "leader" of each meeting be consciously attentive to this.) It is especially recommended that the facilitator **remind** the group at the beginning of the meeting that the focus of both presentation and discussion should be more on the presenter than on the situation, and that the basic intent of the meeting is to be open and responsive to the Holy Spirit. The agenda for each group meeting and time allotted to each portion of it, to be monitored by the facilitator, should be approximately as follows:

1. Opening—by facilitator (including reminding group about the intended focus and attitude).

2. Silence—with or without a reading, music, or spoken prayer, 15 minutes, led by facilitator.

3. Faith sharing statements related to ministry by people other than the presenter—up to 15 minutes.

4. Presentation—up to 15 minutes (others listen silently; if the presenter has not talked about his/her prayer in relation to what is being presented, the facilitator may ask about this before the presentation is concluded).

5. A few moments for questions of clarification only.

6. Silent prayer, reflection and writing—2 to 3 minutes.

7. Discussion—30 minutes.

8. Process of meeting—10 minutes.*

9. Silence—2 to 5 minutes with or without spoken prayer.

10. Closing—reminding people of next meeting date and settling on facilitator and presenter.

*Item #8, the "process of meeting," involves the facilitator asking the group to reflect on the sense of prayerful presence within the group, noting what facilitated that or seemed to get in the way. Was there a sense of spiritual direction happening for the presenter in the group, from the standpoint of group members? Questions like these may be helpful for this discussion:

1. How well did I/we stay focused on the presenter? (as opposed to the situation)

2. Any special places where I/we seemed to be "off track"? (e.g. too much problem-solving, overly analytical, not attentive to the Spirit)

3. What was the quality of silence, attention to God in the group?

The presenter might share his or her perceptions of the discussion—the sense of it as spiritual direction, including anything that seemed to be especially on target, a particular "nudge of grace" in the presence or words of others.

III. Some Questions To Reflect Upon in the Group

For many people, this kind of group meeting is very unusual, and it may take some getting used to. To help with this, members might consider asking the kinds of questions listed below. These are grouped under four major headings: Prayer, the Situation, the Presenter, and Discernment. Each of these areas should probably be addressed in some way in every discussion. You will find it worthwhile to review these questions from time to time to make sure the group is not tending to ignore any of the four areas these questions cover.

Questions About Prayer

How does the presenter pray for or about the situation? What happens?

How much does the presenter actually know about the people involved in the situation? Have they prayed together? shared faith together?

How much does the group know about the presenter's way of relating to God? How might the presenter's way of relating to God affect his/her way of relating to people in the situation?

How does prayer enter into the situation? Does the presenter pray with those involved in the situation? Silently? Aloud? Do they have an agreement to pray for each other?

What are the presenter's experiences of and assumptions about the way God is present in the situation?

Questions About the Situation/Ministry

What are the expectations of the people involved in this situation/ministry regarding the presenter? Does this seem to be clear to all involved?

What expectations or hopes does the presenter have for himself/herself in this situation/ministry? Have these been made explicit with God? with those involved?

Is there an opportunity within the work setting for the presenter to discuss the situation or the ministry itself with co-ministers? Has the presenter taken advantage of this opportunity? If not, why not?

How does the presenter see God active in this situation and in the ministry itself?

What seem to be signs of grace in the situation? How does the situation seem to be a "gift" for the presenter, and vice versa?

How does the presenter feel before and after having been in this situation? or about the ministry itself?

Within the presented situation, is there some threat or challenge to the presenter's values, beliefs, or psychological adjustment? How might this be affecting the presenter's freedom in the situation?

Are there issues of dependency, attachment, sexuality, anger, power or manipulation that might need to be addressed? Are they seen as obstacles or invitations to growth?

Does there truly seem to be a graced call for the presenter to continue in this situation/this ministry? If so, what are the signs of this? Any indications to consider moving out of the situation/the ministry?

Questions About the Presenter in the Situation

With what sort of attitude does the presenter enter the situation? With what kind of preparation?

What is the nature and quality of the presenter's moment-by-moment awareness of or attention to God while in the situation/ministry?

What was the quality of that awareness while the presenter was presenting the situation?

In the situation, what seems to most help and hinder the presenter's attentiveness to God?

How well can the presenter confront issues in the situation that might be uncomfortable? Can the presenter say the necessary "hard things"?

How does the presenter address the role of the church, of the community, of the body of Christ and of social justice in this situation/ministry?

What is the nature of the presenter's love/compassion in this situation/ministry?

How is the presenter ministered to in this situation/ministry?

How deeply can the presenter touch into the heart of the situation, seeing through personalities, conflicts, and emotions to God's presence in the situation/ministry?

What is the nature of the presenter's confidence? (e.g. Lack of personal confidence causing undue hesitancy? Over-confidence in self causing avoidance of the absolute power of God?

Courageous humility encouraging personal surrender to trust in God for the sake of the situation/the ministry?)

Is the presenter having difficulty or excessive self-consciousness because of "trying to do it right"? If so, can the group help him or her to relax and trust more?

Questions About Discernment

How does the presenter see his or her discernment happening in this situation? How does the presenter seek the guidance of the Holy Spirit and the input of others in this situation? Are there any available sources of truth that the presenter continuously shuts out of the discernment?

How much freedom does the presenter seem to have in responding to the Spirit with the situation?

What evidence does the presenter give of being specifically aware of the workings of grace or the Holy Spirit in the situation?

How relaxed or tense does the presenter seem to be in this situation? What is the presenter's degree of trust in God as contrasted with reliance upon his or her own personal competence and willful effort?

How surrendered is the presenter? Is this a surrender to God? To self? To the situation? To the expectations of others?

Notes

FRONT MATTER

[1] Thomas Kelly. *A Testament of Devotion*. NY: Harper and Row, 1941, p. 46.

INTRODUCTION

[1] See resources such as:

William Barry and William Connolly. *The Practice of Spiritual Direction*. Seabury Press, 1982.

Tilden Edwards. *Spiritual Friend: Reclaiming the Gift of Spiritual Direction*. Paulist Press, 1980.

Carolyn Gratton. *The Art of Spiritual Direction*. Crossroad, 1992.

Margaret Guenther. *Holy Listening: The Art of Spiritual Direction*. Cowley Press, 1992.

[2] Lisa Meyers. "Spiritual Guidance and Small Groups in the Presbyterian and Reformed Tradition." This unpublished paper was written as part of the requirement for the completion of her work for the Spiritual Guidance Program of Shalem Institute.

[3] Donna Lord. "An Experience of Group Direction," *Review for Religious*, Vol. 46, #2, March/April 1987.

[4] Kathleen Fischer. *Women at the Well: Feminist Perspectives on Spiritual Direction*. Paulist Press, 1988.

[5] Lowell Glendon. "Spiritual Direction: A Model for Group

Supervision," in *The Art of Clinical Supervision.* (Barry Estadt, John Compton, and Melvin Blanchette, eds.) Paulist Press, 1987.

⁶ Douglas Steere, ed. *Quaker Spirituality: Selected Writings.* Paulist Press, 1984, pp. 3–53, 312–316.

⁷ George Montague. *The Holy Spirit: Growth of a Biblical Tradition.* Paulist Press, 1976, chs. 13-15.

⁸ David W. Johnson and Frank P. Johnson. *Joining Together: Group Theory and Group Skills.* Prentice-Hall, 1982.

Rodney Napier and Matti Gershenfeld. *Groups: Theory and Experience.* Houghton Mifflin Company, 1987.

Irvin Yalom. *The Theory and Practice of Group Psychotherapy.* Basic Books, Inc., 1985.

CHAPTER 1

¹ This and all other passages from scripture are taken from *The New Jerusalem Bible*, Henry Wansbrough, General Editor. Doubleday and Company, 1985.

² Jerome Theisen. *Community and Disunity: Symbols of Grace and Sin.* St. John's University Press, 1985, p. 102.

³ Thich Nhat Hanh. *Peace Is Every Step.* Bantam Press, 1992, pp. 39 and 96.

⁴ Teilhard de Chardin. *The Phenomenon of Man.* Harper Torchbooks, 1961, p. 264.

⁵ Chogyam Trungpa. *The Myth of Freedom.* Shambhala, 1988, p. 103.

⁶ Theisen, p. 110.

⁷ Walter M. Abbott, ed. *The Documents of Vatican II.* The America Press, 1966, pp. 55–72.

[8] Acts 2:42–47.

[9] Rosemary Radford Ruether. "Patristic Spirituality and the Experience of Women in the Early Church," in *Western Spirituality: Historical Roots, Ecumenical Routes*. Fides/Claretian, 1979, pp. 153–155.

[10] John K. Ryan. *Introduction to the Devout Life*, by Saint Francis de Sales. Image Books, 1966, pp. 175–176.

[11] Barbara Bedolla and Dominic Totaro, S.J. "Ignatian Spirituality," in *Spiritual Traditions for the Contemporary Church* by Robin Maas and Gabriel O'Donnell, O.P. Abingdon Press, 1990, Ch. 6, p. 184.

[12] Albert Blatnik. *Your Fourth Day*. National Ultreya Publications, 1973, p. 53.

David Knight. *Cursillo Spiritual Formation Program*. National Ultreya Publications, 1984.

[13] David Watson, *The Early Methodist Class Meeting: Its Origins and Significance*. Discipleship Resources, 1985, p. 20.

Robin Maas, "Wesleyan Spirituality," in *Spiritual Traditions for the Contemporary Church* by Robin Maas and Gabriel O'Donnell, O.P. Abingdon Press, 1990, Ch. 10, pp. 306–308.

[14] Ibid.

[15] David Watson. *Accountable Discipleship: A Handbook for Covenant Discipleship Groups in the Congregation*. 1986, pp. 18 and 19.

[16] Ibid.

[17] Marlene Kropf. "Friends and Lovers: Discipling in a New Key," Unpublished Manuscript for the Congregational Discipling Model Meeting, 1989.

[18] Craig Dykstra, *Growing in the Life of Christian Faith*.

Theology and Worship Ministry Unit, Presbyterian Church (USA), 1989.

[19] Thomas A. Kleissler, Margo A. LeBert, Mary C. McGuinness. *Small Christian Communities: A Vision of Hope.* Paulist Press, 1991, p. 30.

[20] Parker Pa~~l~~ ~~er~~. "The Clearness Committee: A Way of Discernme~~nt~~ ~~~~ *~~i~~ngs*, Vol. 3, #4, l988.

[21] ~~OSB~~, ed. *The Rule of Saint Benedict.*

~~ER 2~~

[1] Jer~~~~ ~~~~ ~~~~d Mary C. Coelho. *Writings in Spiritual Direction~~~~ ~~~~ess*, 1990, p. 90.

[2] Lavini~~a~~ Byrne, IBVM, ed. *Traditions of Spiritual Guidance.* Liturgical Press, 1990, p. 207.

In an essay in this book entitled "Spiritual Guidance in Islam," John Renard, S.J. writes of Ibn Abbad, Islamic spiritual guide: "On the whole, Ibn Abbad's approach to the role of the spiritual guide strikes one as quite balanced. He examines thoroughly in one of his Letters (Letter XVI in 'Letters on the Sufi path') the question of whether or not a seeker actually needs a living guide. He concludes that one does not simply attach oneself to the right shaykh. God alone can provide the gift of a truly sagacious director. God decides whether and when the person will find personal guidance. One ought therefore neither spend too much effort searching, nor simply despair of finding such a guide, but merely be prepared for the gift should it be offered."

In Acts 9:3-19 we read that Saul, later to be called Paul, was directed to go to Ananias for healing and instruction. At the same time, Ananias had been prepared in a vision for Saul's coming and told, with great protest from Ananias, that he should receive Saul.

[3] For further understanding of spiritual direction and other models of direction, you might explore *Traditions of Spiritual Guidance*, edited by Lavinia Byrne, cited above, and also the following:

William Barry and William Connolly. *The Practice of Spiritual Direction*. Seabury Press, 1982.

Dorothy Devers. *Faithful Friendship*. Forward Movement Press, 1980.

Tilden Edwards. *Spiritual Friend*. Paulist Press, 1980.

Carolyn Gratton. *The Art of Spiritual Guidance*. Crossroad, 1992.

Margaret Guenther. *Holy Listening: The Art of Spiritual Direction*. Cowley Press, 1992, especially Chapter 3.

[4] In the Buddhist sense of transmission when a person goes to a guru to seek truth, both the disciple and the guru act as an entrance to that truth, and so a deeper truth emerges for both. See *Meditation in Action* by Chogyam Trungpa. Shambhala Press, 1969, p. 33.

[5] 1 Kings 19:11-13.

[6] Michael Barnes, S.J. "The Guru in Hinduism," in *Traditions of Spiritual Guidance*, p. 173, Lavinia Byrne, IBVM, ed.

CHAPTER 3

[1] Andrew Wilson, ed. *World Scripture: A Comparative Anthology of Sacred Texts*. Paragon House, 1991, p. 187.

[2] *World Scripture: A Comparative Anthology of Sacred Texts*, p. 382.

[3] Swami Nikhilanada, ed. *The Spiritual Heritage of India*. Vedanda Press, 1963, p. 381.

[4] Katsuki Sekida, trans. *Two Zen Classics: Mumonkan and Hekiganroku*. Weatherhill: 1977, p. 383.

[5] 1 Corinthians 2:7-10.

[6] Joseph Chilton Pearce. "Finding Our Dharma," in *Darshan: Dharma, The Natural Law*, #15, June, 1988.

[7] Louis J. Puhl, S.J. *The Spiritual Exercises of Saint Ignatius*. Loyola University Press, 1951.

David L. Fleming, S.J. *The Christian Ministry of Spiritual Direction*. Review for Religious, 1988, sections V, B and C.

John of the Cross. "The Ascent of Mt. Carmel," pp. 67-292; "The Dark Night," pp. 295-389, in *The Collected Work of John of the Cross*. Kieran Kavanaugh, OCD and Otilio Rodriguez, OCD, trans. Institute of Carmelite Studies, 1973.

Teresa of Avila. "The Interior Castle," in *The Collected Works of Teresa of Avila*, vol. 2. Kieran Kavanaugh, OCD and Otilio Rodriguez, OCD, trans. Institute of Carmelite Studies, 1980.

Thomas Green. *Weeds Among the Wheat*. Ave Maria Press, 1984.

[8] C.S. Lewis. *The Screwtape Letters*. Macmillan Publishing Company, 1982, pp. 21, 23.

[9] Laszlo Slomovits. "Old Lovers," in *The Long Journey Called Home*. ASCAP, 1976.

[10] Joan M. Nuth. *Wisdom's Daughter: The Theology of Julian of Norwich*. Crossroad Publishing Company, 1991, especially part two.

[11] From Fr. Provincial's Address to Maryland Province Jesuits, 1980.

[12] Thomas Kelly. *Testament of Devotion*, p. 118.

CHAPTER 4

[1] Carolyn Gratton. *The Art of Spiritual Guidance*. The Crossroad Publishing Company, 1992, p. 143.

[2] Margaret Dorgan, D.C.M. *Guidance in Prayer from Three Women Mystics: Julian of Norwich, Teresa of Avila, Therese of Lisieux.* Credence Cassettes, 1986.

[3] Thelma Hall. *Too Deep for Words: Rediscovering Lectio Divina.* NY: Paulist Press, 1988.

Martin L. Smith. *The Word Is Very Near You: A Guide to Praying with Scripture*. Cowley Press, 1989.

(Both are excellent resources for praying with Scripture and selecting passages according to themes.)

[4] Jan Johnson. "Journaling: Breathing Space in the Spiritual Journey," *Weavings*, Volume VIII, number 2, pp. 34-41.

Joseph Schmidt. *Praying Our Experiences*. St. Mary's Press, 1989.

[5] Susan Burke. "Group Spiritual Direction" *Shalem News,* Volume VII, Number 1, February, 1993, p. 11.

CHAPTER 5

[1] Edmund Colledge, O.S.A. and James Walsh, S.J., trans. *Julian of Norwich—Showings*. Paulist Press, 1978, p. 193.

[2] For some delineations between spiritual direction and psychological counseling see Gerald May's book, *Care of Mind, Care of Spirit*. HarperSanFrancisco, 1992, Ch. 1.

[3] The following readings may be helpful to facilitators in assisting people to get in touch with and find a language for their faith experience:

William Barry and William Connolly. *The Practice of Spiritual Direction*. Seabury, 1982.

Thomas Hart. *The Art of Christian Listening*. Paulist, 1980.

William Johnston, trans. *Cloud of Unknowing*. Image (Doubleday), 1973.

Joseph Schmidt. *Praying Our Experiences*. St. Mary's Press, 1980.

CHAPTER 6

[1] Thomas Story in *Quaker Spirituality,* edited by Douglas Steere. Paulist Press, 1984, p. 10.

[2] For a discussion of difficulties that may arise in growth groups, see:

David W. Johnson and Frank P. Johnson. *Joining Together— Group Theory and Group Skills*. Prentice-Hall, 1982, Ch. 13.

Rodney Napier and Matti Gershenfeld. *Groups: Theory and Experience*. Houghton Mifflin Company, 1987, Chs. 3 and 9.

Irvin D. Yalom. *The Theory and Practice of Group Psychotherapy*. Basic Books, Inc., 1985, Ch. 10.

[3] People at a given time may approach God primarily through their cognitive/rational minds, feelings, senses, imaginations, intuition, or other ways. These can be reflected through emphasis being given to different spiritual paths, such as the devotional, action, cognitive, or intuitive. For a fuller description of these paths, see Tilden Edwards, Jr. *Spiritual Friend: Reclaiming the Gift of Spiritual Direction*. Paulist Press, 1980, p. 113.

[4] Thomas Story in *Quaker Spirituality*, p. 10.

CHAPTER 7

[1] Wendy M. Wright. "Contemplation in a Time of War," *Weavings*, Volume VII, #4, July/August, 1992.

[2] For a discussion of the value of silence and how it might be introduced in parish settings, see Henri Nouwen's book, *The Way of the Heart*. Seabury Press, 1981, pp. 41-66.

[3] Jeremiah 29:10-14.

[4] John 14:15-21.

[5] The *Little Rock Scripture Study Program*, The Liturgical Press, 1987, offers numerous resources for the personal assimilation of God's Word in Scripture.

[6] For a full description of "Lectio Divina," see *Too Deep for Words*, by Thelma Hall. Paulist Press, 1988.

[7] Patricia Mische of Global Associates, printed source unknown.

[8] For specific practices of hospitable prayer, see Edward Hays' book, *Prayers for a Planetary Pilgrim*. Forest of Peace Books, Inc. 1988, especially p. 262.

[9] Wendy Wright, op. cit.

EPILOGUE

[1] Evelyn Underhill. *The Spiritual Life*. Harper and Row, 1963, p. 99.

[2] John 17:21.

Topical Reading List

(I resonate with the words of Thomas à Kempis, author of the spiritual classic, *The Imitation of Christ*: "I would rather be able to experience compassion than be able to define it." Therefore I am reluctant to suggest a reading list although I realize it will provide resources beyond my text which may be valuable for many. My concern is that readers will feel that they need to explore all the themes of my book in greater detail before they are ready to experience Group Spiritual Direction when, in fact, such premature exploration might somehow detract from the richness of the experience.)

Spiritual Community:

Bonhoeffer, Dietrich. *Life Together*. Harper and Row, 1954.

Kelly, Thomas. *A Testament of Devotion*. Harper and Row, 1941.

Nouwen, Henry. *Reaching Out*. Doubleday and Company, 1976.

Parabola (entire issue), Volume XV11, #1, February, 1992.

Theisen, Jerome. *Community and Disunity: Symbols of Grace and Sin*. St. John's University Press, 1985.

Vanier, Jean. *The Broken Body*. Paulist Press, 1988.

Intercessory Prayer:

Steere, Douglas. "Intercession: Caring for Souls," *Weavings*, Volume 1V, #2, March/April, 1989.

Ulanov, Ann and Barry. *Primary Speech: A Psychology of Prayer.* John Knox Press, 1982, ch. 9.

Underhill, Evelyn. *The Spiritual Life.* Harper and Row, 1963, part 3.

Wink, Walter. "History Belongs to the Intercessors," *Sojourners*, October, 1990.

———. "God Is the Intercessor," *Sojourners*, November, 1990.

Building Small Faith Communities:

Bangham, William. *The Journey into Small Groups.* Brotherhood Commission, 1974.

Baranowski, Arthur R. *Called To Be Church.* St. Anthony Messenger Press, 1988.

Dykstra, Craig. *Growing in the Life of Christian Faith.* Theology and Worship Ministry Unit, Presbyterian Church (USA), 1989.

Kleissler, Thomas A., Margo A. LeBert, Mary C. McGuinness. *Small Christian Communities: A Vision of Hope.* Paulist Press, 1991.

Little Rock Scripture Study Program. The Liturgical Press, 1987.

Olsen, Charles. *Cultivating Religious Growth Groups.* Westminster Press, 1984.

Martin, John R. *Ventures in Discipleship.* Herald Press, 1984.

Watson, David. *Accountable Discipleship: A Handbook for Covenant Discipleship Groups in the Congregation.* The Upper Room, 1986.

Westley, Dick. *Good Things Happen: Experiencing Community in Small Groups.* Twenty-Third Publications, 1992.

Spiritual Direction:

Barry, William and William Connolly. *The Practice of Spiritual Direction*. Harper and Row (Seabury Press), 1982.

Byrne, Lavinia, IBVM, ed. *Traditions of Spiritual Guidance*. Liturgical Press, 1990.

Gratton, Carolyn. *The Art of Spiritual Guidance*. Crossroad, 1992.

Hart Thomas. *The Art of Christian Listening*. Paulist, 1980.

Group Spiritual Direction:

Lord, Donna. "An Experience of Group Direction," *Review for Religious*, Volume 46, #2, March/April, 1987.

Discernment:

Barry, William, S.J. *Paying Attention to God*. Notre Dame, 1990.

de Caussade, Jean-Pierre. *The Sacrament of the Present Moment*. Harper and Row, 1989.

Farnham, Suzanne. *Listening Hearts*. The Morehouse Publishing Co., 1991.

Kelly, Thomas. *A Testament of Devotion*. Harper and Row, 1941, pp. 29-76.

Lewis, C.S. *The Screwtape Letters*. Macmillan Publishing Company, 1982.

Contemplative Prayer and Practice:

Edwards, Tilden. *Living in the Presence: Disciplines for the Spiritual Heart*. Harper and Row, 1995.

Hall, Thelma. *Too Deep for Words: Rediscovering Lectio Divina.* Paulist Press, 1988.

Hanh, Thich Nhat. *Peace Is Every Step.* Bantam, 1992.

Hays, Edward. *Prayers for a Planetary Pilgrim.* Forest of Peace, Inc., 1989.

Jager, Willigis. *The Way to Contemplation.* Paulist Press, 1987.

Weavings (entire issue), Volume V11, #4, July/August, 1992.

Psychological Dimensions of the Spiritual Direction Relationship:

May, Gerald. *Care of Mind/Care of Spirit.* HarperSanFrancisco, 1992.

Rohr, Richard. "Why Does Psychology Always Win?" *Sojourners*, November, 1991.

Learnings from Group Therapy and Group Theory That May Be Relevant to Groups for Spiritual Direction:

Egan, Gerard. *You and Me: The Skills of Communicating and Relating to Others.* Wadsworth Publishing Co., 1977.

Johnson, David W. and Frank P. Johnson. *Joining Together: Group Theory and Group Skills.* Prentice-Hall, 1982, ch. 13.

Napier, Rodney and Matti Gershenfeld. *Groups: Theory and Experience.* Houghton Mifflin Company, 1987, chs. 3, 9.

Yalom, Irvin D. *The Theory and Practice of Group Psychotherapy.* Basic Books, Inc., 1985, chs. 1, 10.

Bibliography

Abbott, Walter M., ed. *The Documents of Vatican II*. The America Press, 1966.

Barnes, Michael, S.J. "The Guru in Hinduism," in *Traditions of Spiritual Guidance*. Byrne, Lavinia, IBVM, ed. Liturgical Press, 1990.

Barry, William and William Connolly. *The Practice of Spiritual Direction*. Harper & Row (Seabury Press), 1982.

Bedolla, Barbara and Dominic Totaro, S.J. "Ignatian Spirituality," in *Spiritual Traditions for the Contempory Church*. Robin Maas and Gabriel O'Donnell, O.P., eds. Abingdon Press, 1990.

Bonnin, Eduardo. *Cursillos in Christianity: The How and The Why*. National Ultreya Publications, 1981.

Burke, Susan. "Group Spiritual Direction," *Shalem News*, Volume V11, #1, February, 1993.

Chittister, Joan D., O.S.B., ed. *The Rule of Saint Benedict*. Crossroad, 1992.

Chogyam Trungpa. *Meditation in Action*. Shambhala Press, 1969.

————. *The Myth of Freedom*. Shambhala Press, 1988.

De Chardin, Teilard. *The Phenomenon of Man*. Harper Torchbooks, 1961.

Devers, Dorothy. *Faithful Friendship*. Forward Movement Press, 1980.

Dorgan, Margaret, D.C.M. *Guidance in Prayer from Three Women Mystics: Julian of Norwich, Teresa of Avila, Therese of Lisieux*. Credence Cassettes, 1986.

Dykstra, Craig. *Growing in the Life of Christian Faith*. Theology and Worship Ministry Unit, Presbyterian Church (USA), 1989.

Edwards, Tilden, Jr. *Living in the Presence: Disciplines for the Spiritual Heart*. Harper and Row, 1995.

_____. *Spiritual Friend: Reclaiming the Gift of Spiritual Direction*. Paulist Press, 1980.

Fischer, Kathleen. *Women at the Well: Feminist Perspectives on Spiritual Direction*. Paulist Press, 1988.

Fleming, David L., S.J. *The Christian Ministry of Spiritual Direction*. Review for Religious, 1988.

Glendon, Lowell. "Spiritual Direction: A Model for Group Supervision," in *The Art of Clinical Supervision*. Barry Estadt, John Compton, and Melvin Blanchette, eds. Paulist Press, 1987.

Gratton, Carolyn. *The Art of Spiritual Guidance*. Crossroad, 1992.

Green, Thomas. *Weeds Among the Wheat*. Ave Maria Press, 1984.

Guenther, Margaret. *Holy Listening: The Art of Spiritual Direction*. Cowley Press, 1992.

Hanh, Thich Nhat. *Peace Is Every Step*. Bantam Press, 1992.

Hall, Thelma. *Too Deep for Words: Rediscovering Lectio Divina*. Paulist Press, 1988.

Hart, Thomas. *The Art of Christian Listening*. Paulist Press, 1980.

Hays, Edward. *Prayers for a Planetary Pilgrim*. Forest of Peace Books, Inc., 1988.

John of the Cross. "The Ascent of Mt. Carmel," pp. 67-292; "The Dark Night," pp. 295-389 in *The Collected Work of John of the Cross*. Kieran Kavanaugh, O.C.D. and Otilio Rodriquez, O.C.D., trans. Institute of Carmelite Studies, 1979.

Johnson, David W. and Frank P. Johnson. *Joining Together: Group Theory and Group Skills*. Prentice-Hall, 1982.

Johnson, Jan. "Journaling: Breathing Space in the Spiritual Journey," *Weavings*, Volume VIII, #2.

Johnston, William, trans. *Cloud of Unknowing*. Image (Doubleday), 1973.

Kelly, Thomas. *A Testament of Devotion*. Harper and Row, 1941.

Kleeissler, Thomas A., Margo A. LeBert, Mary C. McGuinness. *Small Christian Communities: A Vision of Hope*. Paulist Press, 1991.

Kropf, Marlene. "Friends and Lovers: Discipling in a New Key," Unpublished Manuscript for the Congregational Discipling Model Meeting, 1989.

Lewis, C.S. *The Screwtape Letters*. Macmillan Publishing Company, 1982.

Little Rock Scripture Study Program. The Liturgical Press, 1987.

Lord, Donna. "An Experience of Group Direction," *Review for Religious*, Volume 46, #2, March/April, 1987.

Maas, Robin. "Wesleyan Spirituality," in *Spiritual Traditions for the Contemporary Church*, Robin Maas and Gabriel O'Donnell, O.P., eds. Abingdon Press, 1990.

Martin, John R. *Ventures in Discipleship*. Herald Press, 1984.

May, Gerald. *Care of Mind/Care of Spirit*. HarperSanFrancisco, 1992.

Meyers, Lisa. "Spiritual Guidance and Small Groups in the Presbyterian and Reformed Tradition." Unpublished paper written as part of the requirement for the completion of her work for the Spiritual Guidance Program of Shalem Institute, 1991.

Montague, George. *The Holy Spirit: Growth of a Biblical Tradition*. Paulist Press, 1976.

Napier, Rodney and Matti Gershenfeld. *Groups: Theory and Experience*. Houghton Mifflin Company, 1987.

Neufelder, Jerome, and Mary C. Coelho. *Writings in Spiritual Direction*. Seabury Press, 1982.

Nouwen, Henri. *The Way of the Heart*. Seabury Press, 1981, pp. 41-66.

Nuth, Joan M. *Wisdom's Daughter: The Theology of Julian of Norwich*. Crossroad Publishing Company, 1991.

Olsen, Charles. *Cultivating Religious Growth Groups*. Westminster Press, 1984.

Palmer, Parker. "The Clearness Committee: A Way of Discernment," *Weavings*, Volume 3, #4, 1988.

Pearce, Joseph Chilton. "Finding Our Dharma," *Darshan: Dharma, The Natural Law*, #15, June, 1988.

Puhl, Louis J., S.J. *The Spiritual Exercises of Saint Ignatius*. Loyola University Press, 1951.

Renard, John, S.J. "Spiritual Guidance in Islam," in *Traditions of Spiritual Guidance*. Byrne, Lavinia, IBVM, ed. Liturgical Press 1990.

Ruether, Rosemary Radford. "Patristic Spirituality and the

Experience of Women in the Early Church," in *Western Spirituality: Historical Roots, Ecumenical Routes.* Fides/Claretian, 1979.

Ryan, John K., trans. *Introduction to the Devout Life*, by Saint Francis de Sales. Image Books, 1966.

Schmidt, Joseph. *Praying Our Experiences.* St. Mary's Press, 1989.

Sekida Katsuki, trans. *Two Zen Classics: Mumonkan and Hekiganroku.* Weatherhill, 1977.

Slomovits, Laszlo. "Old Lovers," in *The Long Journey Called Home.* ASCAP, 1976.

Smith, Martin L. *The Word Is Very Near You: A Guide to Praying with Scripture.* Cowley Press, 1989.

Steere, Douglas. *Quaker Spirituality: Selected Writings.* Paulist Press, 1984.

Swami Nikhilanada, ed. *The Spiritual Heritage of India.* Vedanda Press, 1963.

Teresa of Avila. "The Interior Castle," in *The Collected Works of Teresa of Avila*, Volume 2. Kieran Kavanaugh, OCD, and Otilio Rodriquez, OCD, trans. Institute of Carmelite Studies, 1980.

Theisen, Jerome. *Community and Disunity: Symbols of Grace and Sin.* St. John's University Press, 1985.

Underhill, Evelyn. *The Spiritual Life.* Harper and Row, 1963.

Wansbrough, Henry, general editor. *The New Jerusalem Bible.* Doubleday and Company, 1985.

Watson, David. *The Early Methodist Class Meeting: Its Origins and Significance.* Discipleship Resources, 1985.

_____. *Accountable Discipleship: A Handbook for Covenant*

Discipleship Groups in the Congregation. Discipleship Resources, 1986.

Wilson, Andrew, ed. *World Scripture: A Comparative Anthology of Sacred Texts.* Paragon House, 1991.

Wright, Wendy M. "Contemplation in a Time of War," *Weavings*, Volume VII, #4, July/August, 1992.

Yalom, Irvin D. *The Theory and Practice of Group Psychotherapy.* Basic Books, Inc., 1985.